THE LIFE AND POEMS OF
WILLIAM CARTWRIGHT

CAMBRIDGE UNIVERSITY PRESS
C. F. CLAY, MANAGER

LONDON
FETTER LANE, E.C. 4

EDINBURGH
100 PRINCES STREET

NEW YORK: G. P. PUTNAM'S SONS
BOMBAY, CALCUTTA, MADRAS: MACMILLAN AND CO., LTD.
TORONTO: J. M. DENT AND SONS, LTD.
TOKYO: THE MARUZEN-KABUSHIKI-KAISHA

THE LIFE AND POEMS OF WILLIAM CARTWRIGHT

EDITED BY

R. CULLIS GOFFIN, M.A.

INDIAN EDUCATIONAL SERVICE

CAMBRIDGE :
AT THE UNIVERSITY PRESS
1918

TO

MY BROTHER

BORN : VIZIANAGRAM, INDIA, 4 FEB. 1887,
KILLED : YPRES, BELGIUM, 4 JUNE, 1915.

PREFACE

READERS of Cartwright will agree that this spirited and once famous writer has been too long neglected. His poems have been arranged, generally speaking, in the order in which they appear in the rare 1651 Edition of Cartwright's Plays and Poems (*v.* Introd. p. xl and xliv). The Songs from the Plays contained in that Edition have also been included here.

In annotating the poems, I have tried to avoid too much "blanching the obscure places and discourse upon the plain." But it is inevitable that such work should appear capricious to some.

I am grateful to Prof. W. P. Ker for suggesting this subject to me as one of promise; and, while he is in no way responsible for what this book contains, for his help and advice in my work upon it; to Dr R. W. Chambers for time always placed ungrudgingly at my disposal; to the Cambridge University Press reader who has set right certain MS. errors; and finally, to my father, the Rev. H. J. Goffin, for his undertaking on my behalf to see the volume through the press. *Gloria filiorum patres!*

R. C. G.

GAUHATI, ASSAM.
October, 1916.

CONTENTS

INTRODUCTION

" WILLIAM CARTWRIGHT, the most noted poet, orator and philosopher of his time, was born at Northway, near Tewkesbury in Gloucestershire, in September, 1611 (9 Jac. I), and baptized there on the 26th day of the same month." So runs the account given by Anthony à Wood in the *Athenae Oxonienses*. But Lloyd had given a different story in his *Memoirs*. He speaks there of "Mr Wm. Cartwright, Son of Thomas Cartwright of Burford, in the County of Oxford, born August 16. 1615."

There is a note added to Wood's account to be found in Bliss's edition of the *Athenae*.

"Although I had no doubt," says Bliss, "as to Wood's accuracy, I was induced to write to Burford in order, if possible, to satisfy my readers on this point, and I have been favoured by the Rev. Francis Knollis, vicar of Burford, with a letter on the subject, from which I extract the following: 'I have very carefully examined the register of Burford, but can find no such name as that of *Cartwright*, and therefore conclude that no family of that name did reside here. I have likewise examined the register of the chapelry of Fulbrook, but without success.'

"Lloyd is not, by any means, a writer to be depended

on, as Wood well knew, when he gave him the character
to be found in another part of this work, and I was in
great hopes that I might have proved my author's correct-
ness by an application at Northway; here, however,
unfortunately (as I learn by the kindness of the Rev.
D. C. Parry) the early registers are lost, but, says Mr Parry,
'I was informed there were strong reasons for believing
that persons of that name (Cartwright) did at some time
live in the hamlet of Northway.' The earliest register,
it seems, commences in 1703, and the name occurs once
only during the first twenty years."

The balance of evidence obviously favours Wood even
at this point. Masson, in his life of Milton, refers to
Cartwright as "the son of a Gloucestershire innkeeper,"
and Welch[1] too follows Wood. But Mr A. H. Bullen in
the *Dictionary of National Biography* only accepts Wood's
account as "probably true."

It was Aubrey who was Wood's authority. Aubrey
knew the Cartwright family personally. That Northway
was the birthplace, "I have from his brother," he says,
"who lives not far from me, and from his sisters whom
I called upon in Gloucestershire in Leckhampton."

Northway, in Gloucestershire, is a hamlet within the
parish of Ashchurch, near Tewkesbury. The registers of
Ashchurch are *not* lost. On the contrary, they go back,
more or less completely, to the year 1555. Under the
year 1611, on the 26th day of December, occurs the entry
of the baptism of a William Cartwright, son of William
Cartwright. His sister Howes, mentioned by Aubrey,
was born four years later.

---

[1] In his *Alumni Westmonasterienses*.

Both his father and his uncle, Thexton Cartwright,
had been to the university of Oxford. The entries in
Foster's *Alumni Oxonienses* are unmistakable:

"*Thekeston C.* of co. Glos. pleb. Ball. Col. matric.
28 June 1604, aged 16; son of Timothy C. of Washborne
co. Glos. (and his wife, d. of Sir John Thexton of London),
brother of Wm. of same date.

"*Wm. C.* of co. Glos. pleb. Balliol Col. matric. 28 June
1604, aged 18; married Dorothy, daughter of Rowland
Coles, of Northway, possibly [*sic*] father of the next named,
brother of Thexton, or Thekeston, same date."

The poet's uncle Thexton is not mentioned in the family
tree (see p. xiv below); at any rate, here is some evidence
of the family learning. Later follows:

"*Wm. C.* s. Wm. of Heckhampton, co. Glos. gent., etc.
...born at Northway, near Tewkesbury"...(here follow the
dates and successes of the poet).

Also mentioned is a

"*Thos. C.* s. William, of Greekeland, co. Glos. gent.
Ch. Ch. matric. 21 Oct. 1642, aged 16[1]."

The affairs of William Cartwright the elder were then
flourishing. In *Men and Armour for Gloucestershire in
1608*[2] reference is made to him, William Cartwright of
Washborne in Gloucestershire[3], who had two able-bodied
menservants. He is further declared to have been then
about twenty years of age (*i.e.* to have been born about
1588). The dates thus coincide.

[1] The last named Thomas, who also went to Christ Church, may be
a young brother of the poet. And "Greekeland" may be Greet, a
hamlet near Washborne.

[2] Sub cap. *Washborne.*

[3] There *is* another William Cartwright mentioned (sub cap. *Tewkesbury*), of the same age too, a glover.

The family of the Cartwrights was well known in the neighbourhood of Tewkesbury. In Treddington Church (some two and a half miles south-east of Tewkesbury) are inscriptions to several of their family. Rudder, in his *History of Gloucestershire* (p. 235), gives illustrations of the coat of arms of this branch, and it is almost identical with that recorded by the heraldic visitation of the county in 1623. The genealogical table of the Washborne Cartwrights is there[1] given as follows:

Wm. Cartwright of Washborne (Glos.)=d. of Sir Alexander Charlton, Kt.

Penelopye d. of Sir Wm. Segar = Timothy Cartwright = El. d. of Sir Jo. Thexton
Kt. al's Garter princ. K. of | of Washborne 1623 | of London Kt.
Armes

Timothy C. = Margaret d.   Wm. C. = Dorothy   Alice   Margery
      of Thos.   d. of   vx. Robt.   vx. Edwd.
      Deeues   Rowland   Higgs of   Holinden
                Coles of   Chel. 21 y. of London,
                Northway   to Anthony   Grocer
                in co. Glos. Partridge[2]

Thos. C. 1 yere old   Wm. Cartw. 13 yrs.   Thexton Ca.
& more aº. 1623   old 1623

The William last mentioned is evidently the poet. He was born in 1611, and his father's Christian name is the same. His mother, *née* Dorothy Coles, came from Northway, some five miles west of Great Washborne. Her family evidently take recognised rank in that neighbourhood, and their own genealogical tree appears also in the same publication[3].

[1] *Harleian Society Publications, Visitation of Gloucestershire*, 1623.

[2] An account of the marriage agreement between the two Timothy C.'s and Anthony Partridge, who possessed large estates, may be seen in *Glos. Inquis. Post Mortem Chas. I*, p. 2, No. 97, 2100 d. 7.

[3] And see also *Men and Armour*, sub Northway: "Rowland Cole, 'a subsidy man with three servants, unable in body.'"

The elder William belongs to a younger branch of the family; Timothy and after him the infant Thomas both stand in the way of his inheritance. So, it seems, he solves the problem of the lack of prospects by marrying Miss Coles, an heiress in a small way. She brings to him as dowry a hundred pounds a year, and, according to Aubrey, property in Wiltshire. This property was ultimately inherited by William the poet. The married couple then live on land belonging to her family in Northway, and here the poet is born in 1611. Wood describes the poet's father as "once a gentleman of fair estate"; "of three hundred pounds a year," says Aubrey.

Now follows an extraordinary change of fortune. Whether it was due to his lack of private means or to subsequent disaster we do not know, but we next hear of the elder William as an innkeeper near Cirencester. This plunge into business was, according to Wood, made in order to retrieve his broken fortunes. But it only lasted "a year or thereabout," for "he declined and lost by it too[1]."

Wood proceeds to describe how the father, nevertheless, although "living in a middle condition, caused that his son, of great hopes, to be educated under Mr Will. Topp, master of the free school there," *i.e.* in Cirencester. Lloyd omits all mention of this part of Cartwright's education, of Topp's name, and of other details; Wood is evidently the better informed. The name of the schoolmaster, however, appears to have been *Henry*, not *William* Topp. Henry Topp is mentioned by Wood, as a Master of Arts of Oriel College. He was appointed to Cirencester in 1622, and appears, from all accounts, to have had a much better

---

[1] Aubrey.

record as student than as teacher[1]. The abilities of his young pupil William, however, seem to have won recognition. The boy was about eleven years of age when he entered the school. "But so great a progress did he make in a short time, that by the advice of friends, his father got him to be sped a king's scholar at Westminster, compleating his former learning to a miracle under Mr Lambert Osbaldstone." Osbaldstone had been headmaster of Westminster school since 1625; in all he had been there since 1621. His learning was universally admitted; Cowley dedicated a poem to him, calling him "my very loving Master." After what was, evidently, a brilliant career at Westminster, Cartwright was elected student of Christ Church, and went to Oxford. It is a remarkable fact that to this college was being gradually gathered quite a coterie of aspirants to poetic fame; "Christchurch for poets," says one contemporary. His tutor there was Jerumael Terrent, an old Westminster boy himself. Cartwright's tutor has also been identified, but unreasonably, I think, with the *Thomas* Terrent who contributed excellent Latin verses to the *Jonsonus Virbius*.

Cartwright was a brilliant and most industrious student, "sitting sixteen hours a day at all manner of knowledge," says Lloyd in his *Memoirs*. Jasper Mayne thus addresses him in one of the commendatory poems prefixed to the 1651 collected edition of Cartwright's works:

> [Thou] didst run
> A course in knowledge dayly like the Sun,
> And nightly too; For when all other eyes
> Were lock't, and shut, but those that watch the Skies,

[1] Vide *The Victoria History of the County of Gloucester* (Constable, 1907).

Thou, like Discoverers at Sea, went'st on,
To find out new worlds, to all else unknown.
Nor would Thy busie Candle let Thee sleep,
Till Thou had'st fathom'd the unfathom'd Deep.

Wood, too, says he "went through the classes of logic and philosophy with an unwearied industry." During his fifteen years' residence at Oxford Cartwright identified himself with the life of his College and University in all its aspects. He was one of the leaders of the Christ Church students in a protestation to the King against the discipline maintained by the Dean and Chapter[1]. Griffith in his *Praelogium* includes Cartwright among the "numina Oxonii tutelaria[2]." He took his B.A. the 5th June, 1632, and his M.A. the 15th April, 1635. He entered holy orders, became reader in metaphysics, and, finally, proctor in 1643. Yet "his high abilities were accompanied with so much candour and sweetness that they made him equally loved and admired[3]." His oratory, notably in his lectures on the Passions, was highly esteemed in Christ Church. "Those wild beasts (the Passions)," says Lloyd[4], "being tuned and composed to tameness and order, by his sweet and harmonious language," seemed "but varieated reason." His Metaphysic School was continually thronged[5], Oxford at that time being more than ever interested and even concerned in such discussions. Aristotle, under his interpretation, "ran as smooth as Virgil"; his philosophy was "as melting as his plays." "The Theatre was thin

---

[1] *Clarendon State Papers (Domestic)*, 1629, Nov. 17, and 1640-1, Feb. 15.   [2] Wood, *Athenae*, III, 454.

[3] From the Preface to the 1651 edition.

[4] The same phrasing is found in Cartwright's poem *To Mrs Ashford*: "Passions like wilder beasts thus tamèd be."

[5] Moseley corroborates this in his *Preface to the Reader*.

to his school, and Comedy was not half so good entertainment as his Philosophy." "Cartwright was the utmost man could come to," said Dr Fell, not without reason. Meanwhile, perhaps, the poet was able to revive something of his father's old rank. An estate was bought at Leckhampton, near Cheltenham, Gloucestershire. Here the Cartwright family were visited later by Aubrey; this is evidently the place meant by the "Heckhampton" of the *Alumni Oxonienses.*

Politics possessed always a great attraction for Cartwright. He remained an unflinching Royalist until his death, and his own personal devotion to his sovereign is displayed equally in his life and in his verse. All this lay in line with his lifelong attachment to Dr Brian Duppa, likewise an old Westminster boy, who became Dean of Christ Church in 1629. Cartwright, no doubt, owed much of his advancement to the friendship and patronage of this eminent divine, who became Vice-Chancellor in 1632, was private tutor to the Prince of Wales, and in close touch with Archbishop Laud. Many of Cartwright's poems are dedicated to Duppa. The King and Queen, too, were constantly at Oxford, and the life of the Royal family was the great source of inspiration for topical verse-exercises by the scholars. Collections of these academic verse-addresses were made and presented to Royalty whenever occasion offered.

Such a collection was the *Britanniae Natalis,* celebrating the birth of Charles II in 1630, and Cartwright wrote a poem for it in Latin.

Laud, as Chancellor, interfered a good deal with University affairs, and discipline under his authority was strictly enforced. His prohibition of the "Westminster

supper" held on Fridays by the old boys of that school
in Christ Church is typical, and would affect Cartwright[1]. His overshadowing personality is reflected also
in the increasing theological quarrels. Cartwright himself
was, like Duppa, a whole-hearted Laudian; he hated
Puritanism violently; he was a great admirer of Arminius.
Both in his plays and in his verses are many and warm
references to the theological differences and debates of
his day. We can see his familiarity with the technical
terms required for these discussions. His entire devotion
to Laud, that thorough if tactless archbishop, the "gracious
hand who perfected our statutes," is patent enough from
his poems[2].

Cartwright contributed poems in Latin and English
to the ensuing academic collections, as follows:

1631.	*Ad...Iobannen Cirenbergium.*	1 Latin poem.	
1633.	*Pro Rege suo Sotria.*	do.	1 English poem.
„	*Solis Britannici Perigarum.*	do.	do.
„	*Vitis Carolinae Gemma Altera.*	do.	do.

In August, 1636, the King and Queen were entertained
by the University. On the 29th they saw Strode's

---

[1] *Clarendon State Papers 'Domestic'),* 1638, Dec. 20, and see also the
poem *A Bill of Fare,* and note to l. 49, "For, if this fasting hold," etc.

[2] There is an interesting note in Aubrey's *Remains of Gentilisme
and Judaisme* 'ed. Folklore Society from Brit. Mus. MS. 1686-7), p. 69,
which illustrates Cartwright's attitude towards Laud. "When I was
of Trin. Coll. there was a sale of Mr Wm. Cartwright's (Poet) bookes,
many whereof I had; amongst others (I know not how) was Dr Daniel
Featly's *Handmayd to Devotion;* which was printed shortly after
Dr Heylin's Hist. aforesaid. In the Holyday Devotions he speakes
of St George, and asserts the story to be fabulous; and that there was
never any such man. Wm. Cartwright writes in the Margent *'For this
assertion was Dr Featley brought upon his knees before Wm. Laud A-Bp
of Canterbury.'"*

Floating Island produced, with "novel stage appliances," by the students of Christ Church. On the 30th their Majesties witnessed *The Royal Slave*, another "University show" as Ben Jonson called them, written by Cartwright himself. The songs of the play were set to music by Henry Lawes; the "scenic effects," which were reproduced at Hampton Court, were by Inigo Jones.

Cartwright must have been already known as the author of *The Ordinary*. In his prologue to that play he laments his greenness in the ways of the theatre, as well as in those of vice. Moreover, the style of the play and the peculiar zest with which he tries to atone for this inexperience, betray a youthful ambition. Cartwright has, in all, four plays to his name, comedies and tragi-comedies, all printed in the 1651 edition along with the lesser poems. Ward[1] declares them to be "thoroughly rhetorical in manner. The serious dialogue," he says, "is elevated in sentiment, and occasionally graceful in form; but we miss any real play of passion or depth of pathos springing from a truly dramatic imagination. The comic scenes are almost wholly conventional; for of comic power Cartwright seems to have been devoid. More or less absorbed in the life of his university, though under aspects more important than those which occupied Randolph [at Cambridge], Cartwright must have been without the wider experience of men and manners which in a comic dramatist so often serves as a substitute for originality."

The play chosen or written for the King's entertainment was at any rate his most original effort. *The Lady Errant* seems to be founded on an idea taken from Fletcher's *The Sea Voyage*; *The Siedge* is based on an anecdote

[1] In *English Dramatic Literature*, III, p. 139.

related by Plutarch; while *The Ordinary* is a confessedly second-hand study of London rascal society.

The Royal Slave (there are two editions, 1639, and 1640, both at Oxford) was produced with the same mechanical contrivances as had been used with Strode's *Floating Island*. But Cartwright's play contained much more variety. "It was very well penn'd and acted, and the strangeness of the Persian habits gave great content." "All things went happy," said the Chancellor[1]. According to Evelyn, Strode's play was a little too grave and hard to understand. On the other hand Evelyn declares that "His Majesty and all the Nobles" commended *The Royal Slave* as the best play that ever was acted. One of the student-actors (afterwards to become the famous Dr Busby) performed his part so well that he decided thereupon "to commence actor on the public stage[2]." The University spent altogether more than £800 in preparation for this royal visit[3]; every college contributed to and shared in their Majesties' entertainment[4]. *The Royal Slave* was acted again on September 2nd for the benefit of the University and of strangers. In the following November the Queen asked if she might have the Persian costumes, so that her own players might act the play. The costumes were accordingly sent to Hampton Court, and Cartwright himself went to supervise this professional performance by the King's company. It was again an elaborate pro-

---

[1] See Wood, *Athenae*, and the *Clarendon State Papers* (*Domestic*), 1636, Sept. 4.

[2] See Bray's note to Evelyn, I, 421. The names of the other student actors were preserved in the Heber MS. 1043 of *The Royal Slave*. But this has since been lost. See *Notes and Queries*, 3, VIII, 287, and 5, VIII, 447.   [3] See the account in Madan.

[4] Laud's letter to the Vice-Chancellor (1636).

duction[1], but apparently the glamour had passed. Though Cartwright wrote a new prologue and epilogue to grace the occasion, "by all men's confession the Players came short of the Actors[2]." Cartwright received £40 for his pains, and the precious Persian costumes were carefully preserved, at Laud's request, from becoming mere stage properties.

We next hear of Cartwright as again contributing his share to further academic collections of loyal verse. His contributions were as follows:

1636.	*Coronae Carolinae Quadratura*[3],	1 English,	1 Latin poem.
1637.	*Flos Britannicus*	do.	do.
1638.	*Death Repeal'd...*	do.	do.
„	*Charisteria...pro Maria*	do.	do.
1640.	*Horti Carolini Rosa Altera*	do.	
1641.	*Proteleia Anglo-Batava*	do.	do.

In 1640 a second edition of *The Royal Slave* had been published at Oxford.

By this time Laud's authority was beginning to dwindle. The Long Parliament met, and the opposition in the country to his downright policy became more outspoken. He resigned the Chancellorship of Oxford on the 22nd of June, 1641, and was succeeded on July 1st by Philip Herbert, Earl of Pembroke. It is curious to find Cartwright addressing the newcomer in a poem of welcome and congratulation written in his usual fluent style. This was printed and published as a separate leaflet.

Religious differences were at length merging in bitter

---

[1] Described in *Clarendon State Papers (Domestic)*, 1637, April 11.

[2] Wood, *Athenae*.

[3] Details of these are to be found in the notes to the poems.

and violent civil strife. Oxford was at the heart of all the new movements. On the 9th of August, 1642, a public prosecution was read there against the Parliamentary "rebels." The University began to look to her fortifications and her military resources. In a review of all possible recruits for service, Wood describes how "many Scholars appeared." On the 18th the new contingent was drilled again, and "put into array" in the great quadrangle at Christ Church, always the foremost college among the loyalists. Cartwright, no doubt, was prominent and playing an energetic part. "There were a great number of them Masters of Arts, and Divines also" among these scholar-soldiers, we are told. Cartwright was both, and cherished a worshipful devotion to his King.

Meanwhile Oxford town was not showing herself so surely loyal, and trouble was threatening the University from that quarter. Accordingly a convocation was held and letters read from the King. It was decided to appoint "A Delegacy" to superintend. Out of a total of eight elected to serve, two were members of Christ Church. These were William Stuteville and William Cartwright. The "Delegacy," popularly known in the University as "the Council of War," now took command. Reviews and musters were held; drills were organized in various college grounds; £1000 were raised by public subscription.

Lord Say, a Parliamentary captain, approached Oxford with troops and opened negotiations with the town. He quartered his men in Christ Church meadow, and they sneered at "the painted idolatrous windows" of the College. Although on September the 10th several prominent scholars had left Oxford to serve as volunteers under Sir John

Byrone, Cartwright apparently still remained. We can well imagine his annoyance with these uncouth Parliamentarians. But his position was a dangerous one. Lord Say entered Oxford on September the 14th; the next day hidden treasure was discovered in Christ Church, which had been diligently guarded and searched by the Parliamentary troopers. With Stuteville and John Castilion, another fellow-collegian, Cartwright was put in prison. They were accused of "uttering certain words, and the rather for that they had trained among the Scholars." They were, however, released soon after, "upon £200 bail a piece taken for them, but not to remain in the University, unless by order from the Lord Say[1]." King Charles entered Oxford on November the 29th, and the fugitives were then, if not before, able to return, having successfully avoided falling into the hands of the enemy.

In the preceding October, Cartwright had been appointed succentor or subchaunter in the church of Salisbury, under the patronage of Duppa, his good friend still[2]. Cartwright would not accept a resident post away from his University. And Dr Duppa did not wish "to deprive Oxford" of so zealous a servant, or further preferment would undoubtedly have been put in his way.

In this same October the battle of Edgehill took place. It was after this that the King came on to Oxford, and lodged at Christ Church. On this occasion, "at his (the King's) return from Edgehill fight," Cartwright preached a special sermon "by the King's command."

On the 12th of April, 1643, Cartwright was appointed

[1] Wood.

[2] Dr Duppa had been appointed Chancellor of Salisbury in 1634 and Bishop in December, 1641.

Junior Proctor by the University. The King's cause was at its zenith, and Oxford was regarded by Royalists, at any rate, as the capital town of England. The University felt itself free to return somewhat to the old habits of life. When the Queen entered Oxford on July the 14th, she was hailed by the students in the normal academic way, and, not a fortnight after her arrival, the congratulatory collection of poems (*Epibateria*) was published. Cartwright himself contributed,—and likewise a certain Thomas Cartwright, also of Christ Church, and possibly his younger brother—a poem apiece.

The battle of Lansdown was fought in July and is noteworthy from the gallant part played in it by Sir Bevill Grenville, celebrated by the publication, a month later, of a set of "Verses" in his honour. Cartwright gave of his best to this Royalist panegyric, and his contribution is perhaps the most spirited of his poems.

Oxford was thronged by the military and political followers of the King. In January, 1644, Parliament sat in the great hall at Christ Church. All its rooms were appointed for official uses. From July onwards the Queen herself had been in residence there.

Cartwright was probably living out of College. His short career was now nearly over. The town of Oxford had always been in a most insanitary condition, and *A true relation of the taking of Bristol*, published early in 1643, declares that "men die dayly there of a Callenture, being a burning fever." Cartwright's last poem dates from this time—"*November, of Signal Days observed in that month in relation to the Crown and Royal Family*[1]." It was to be a signal month for the young poet too. The

[1] First published as a broadside, and then reprinted in 1671.

"Morbus Campestris" raged more fiercely than ever. "Many Soldiers and Inhabitants, some also belonging to the King's and Queen's court, with a few Scholars, died thereof." Cartwright was of those stricken. He succumbed after a short illness, but his case evidently aroused great concern. The King, amongst others, constantly enquired of his health.

It is generally declared that Cartwright died on the 29th of November, 1643. This is Wood's account, who further states that he "was buried on the first day of December, towards the upper end of the south isle ["north" says Chalmers, followed by Mr Bullen] joyning to the choir of the cathedral of Christ Church[1]." This is curious, for the entry in the Register of Deaths, preserved in the Vestry at Christ Church, runs as follows: "William Cartwright, Student and Proctor, buried Anno Dmi 1643 December 7th." The "7th" in the Register is quite unmistakable. But the tablet to his memory seems to have disappeared. It probably stood, if indeed there ever was one, in the *south* aisle originally, near where the memorial to Bishop King was formerly placed. That is, it was in the second bay (from the east) of the South Choir aisle. There is now a grating where his slab or lozenge should be. It is probable, however, that no inscription to his memory was ever composed; certainly, it was not in those troubled days. "Pitty 'tis so famous a bard should lye without an inscription," declares Aubrey.

---

[1] The lines

>   thy famous Colledge has the trust
>   Preferr'd to be the Wardrobe of thy Dust

occur in the Introductory Verses by R. Gardiner, prefixed to the 1651 edition. And vide also Wood, *Hist. and Antiq.* III, 508.

The King insisted on appearing in mourning on the day
of the funeral. "Since the Muses," said his Majesty, "had
mourned so much for the loss of such a son, it would be a
shame for him not to appear in mourning for the loss of
such a subject." That his King knew and publicly acknow-
ledged his worth and loyalty was the reward Cartwright
himself would most have appreciated. "But what's all
this," says Henry Vaughan[1],

> unto a Royall Test
> *Thou art the Man*, whom great Charles so exprest.

Vaughan evidently felt the sincerity of Cartwright's
homage.

The poems of William Cartwright were collected after
his death and published (in one volume with the plays)
in 1651 by Humphrey Moseley[2]. Moseley at this time enjoyed almost a monopoly in the matter of publishing good
poetry, and appears to have been himself one of the "wits"
of the time. The poems appear in this volume after the
plays, with a sub-heading "The Ayres and Songs set by
Mr Henry Lawes, Servant to his Late Majesty in his
Publick and Private Musick." Lawes himself published
many of his airs, and several of Cartwright's songs, taken
mainly from the plays, appear in these. The music of
The Royal Slave, which added greatly to its popularity,

---

[1] In his poem prefixed to the 1651 edition of Cartwright.

[2] It is a curious fact that this 1651 volume contains no index to
the poems. This is explained by the printer in a postscript: "we
shall not trouble you with an Index; for already the book is bigger
than we meant it, etc." yet "the Bodleian copy contains for fly
leaves fragments of an index to all the poems, which shews that one
was actually printed and suppressed." Wood calls attention to this
paradox in his *Athenae*.

had been specially composed by Lawes. There is nothing
more natural than that Lawes and Cartwright should have
been acquainted; they probably first came together in
1636 in the production of *The Royal Slave* at Christ Church.
They both were of "the society of Ben." Carew, who has
much in common with Cartwright, was a courtier too,
and Lawes and Carew worked up songs and musical enter-
tainments together in the same way. Lawes had from
childhood been in the King's service, and at this period
had reached his highest fame. All the popular poets had
agreed in recognising his abilities as a composer, and as
an adapter of music to verse.

Information about Cartwright may be gleaned not only
from Moseley's *Preface to the Reader*, which begins his
1651 edition of the poet, but also from the host of commendatory poems which form nearly one quarter of the
whole volume. These introductory poems are mainly of a
very conventional inspiration, but they bear unimpeachable
witness to the success and popularity of Cartwright's
muse. Vaughan the Silurist makes his offering:

> Since a Labell fixt to thy fair Hearse
> Is all the mode;

and outside this particular volume, Benlowes, in an introductory poem to his *Theophila*:

> For all these [virtues] died not with fam'd Cartwright though
> A score of poets join'd to have it so;

and Shadwell (in *Bury Fair*, Act ii, Scene 1):

> I, that was a Judge at Blackfriers, writ before *Fletcher's* works and
> *Cartwright's*...and you to say I have no wit,

—all join in the universal tribute (itself becoming a
recognised convention) to Cartwright's renown.

It is remarkable, therefore, to notice that his biographers, both Wood and Lloyd, insist on the solid merits of his character. He was especially beloved, we are told, of those of the gown and of the court, "who esteemed also his life a fair copy of practic piety, a rare example of heroic worth, and in whom arts, learning and language made up the true complement of perfection[1]." His was a magnetic personality. "His soul, naturally great and capable, had ...three advantages to fill it; great spirited Tutors, choice Books and select Company; it was his usual saying, That it was his happiness that he neither heard nor read any thing vulgar, weak or raw, till his mind was fixed to notions exact as reason and as high as fancy....To see...a Miracle of Industry and Wit...turning the Axioms of Aristotle, the problems of Euclide, the summes of Aquinas, the Code of Justinian, the Contexture of History, the learning of Rabbines, the Mythology of Gentilism, the Fathers, Councels, Martyrologyes and Liturgicks and Christians; the Poetry, Oratory, and Criticism of the world into a good Man, a great Scholar, a most ingenious Poet and Orator, and an excellent Preacher, in whom hallowed fancies and reason grew Visions, and holy passions, Raptures and Extasies, and all this at thirty years of age[2]." "All this" was the happy privilege of Cartwright's acquaintance. But allowing for this somewhat "eastern hyperbolical expression" of contemporary admiration, one sees behind it an outline of the truth—that the poet possessed a charming if not a powerful personality, together with many admirable qualities. He himself quietly acquiesced in the general approbation, and with smiling and self-conscious superiority, criticised "the small poets" of

[1] Wood, *Athenae*.   [2] Lloyd, *Memoirs*.

his day[1]. He studied the popular literary taste, and was as self-adapting as Dryden or Defoe. He could write low-life comedy, personal panegyric, or typical seventeenth century love-elegies, with equal ease, in no case identifying himself with what he wrote. He keeps himself detached, as a cultured amateur.

> Troth, I am like small Birds, which now in Spring
> When they have nought to eat, do sit and sing[2].

"These poems were his Recreation," says Moseley. He certainly gave up writing indecent verse when he took Holy Orders, but, in characteristic fashion, he tells us that the new life by no means spells for him the banishment of all the cakes and ale—

> But being the Canon bars me Wit and Wine
> Enjoying the true Vine,

he says, and one suspects a smile at his own virtue. Lines like

> To perish full is not the worst of Fate[3],

and his easy-tempered, somewhat coarse love-poems seem his more natural self-expression.

Cartwright never troubled himself during his short life to collect his verses for publication, although they appear to have enjoyed a wide manuscript circulation. They were, indeed, "so strangely scatter'd that the Printer had difficulty in getting them together[4]." Characteristic

---

[1] In *To John Fletcher* (*Another on the Same*), l. 79. However, he seems to have recognised the fact of the shortness of
the Poets Day:
There's difference between fame, and sudden pay.
    (*To Ben Jonson.*)
[2] From *A Bill of Fare.*   [3] *A Bill of Fare.*
[4] *Preface* to 1651 edition.

poems, like that *To Flora*[1], were overlooked. We learn
one important fact, at least, from the printer's preface to
the 1651 edition—that what he gives us of Cartwright's
work are juvenilia; some were written "before he was
twenty years old, scarce any after five and twenty. Only
one sheet (here included) did he write after entering Holy
Orders [*i.e.* in 1635 or 6]; when he wrote them it was
only to sweeten and relieve deeper thoughts." The historian of English literature must, in view of this statement,
duly weigh Cartwright's claim to originality in both the
subject and form of some of his poems.

Cartwright was one of the "sons" of Ben Jonson. "My
son Cartwright," said Ben, "writes all like a man." The
"son" followed his poetical father in many ways, but
although his verse, at its highest level, approximates to
Jonson's style and standard, he never achieves his master's
unique power of metamorphosing a scholar's notebook
into distinguished poetry with an individual artistic life
of its own. Perhaps Cartwright is closest to Ben in his
play-writing, for there he was playing a purely imitative
game, doubly artificial in the academic. He copied Ben's
liberal use of professional or slang terms, and his free
adaptation of the heroic couplet, not only for dedicatory,
but for minor and occasional poems of all kinds. Cartwright addressed some of his best-known verses to his
master; "my flame," he avowed,

> "Kindled from thine, flies upward tow'rd thy Name[2]."

Cartwright was hailed by the matchless Orinda[3] as a
"Prince of Phansie"; he certainly belonged to the witty

---

[1] Given on p. 34: *A Song of Dalliaunce.*
[2] *To Ben Jonson.*
[3] In the poem subscribed "K.P." included in the 1651 edition.

"metaphysical" school of poetry, and to the fanciful, rather than to the imaginative order of poets. Just as he possessed in his person all the popular virtues, so his poetry contained all the elements which at that time commanded particular admiration. It "committed no trespasses against the Miniver"; it was copious, ingenious, conceited, in short, correct. Hence it repays study, as Chalmers has pointed out, as being so altogether typical of the age.

It is difficult to grasp any unity of "spirit" in the literature of the first half of the seventeenth century. For the progress of poetry from the sixteenth to the eighteenth century was one from *richness* to *clearness* through variety, from roughness to smoothness through experiment, following a line of general simplification in thought and in rhythm. But the Puritans were, as Matthew Arnold has said, as keen on externals as the old Pharisees. So was, indeed, the whole Puritan age. It was a controversial epoch, when the outward religion and the outward character of one's neighbour were studied and debated with the whole-hearted zest of an English village gossip. While Elizabethan life appears national and inward, seventeenth century life seems individual and outward. Hence the difficulty to set down in definition the "spirit" of this age.

There were new schools abroad in poetry. The so-called metaphysical school was one of the many channels into which poetry broke up before its ultimate redintegration. The style of poetry which marked the members of this school was essentially scholarly, and peculiarly compact, with cullings "pressed roughly into service" from the sciences, the arts, and the classics. The watchword of the group was the answer of the academic poet to the challenge of the new "man of letters[1]," and to the vulgarisation of poetic matter and manner which seemed to be menacing the life of ethereal poetry.

The nature and origin of these "metaphysical" aids to the re-enlivenment of poetry have been fully discussed by able and broad-minded historians like Mr Courthope. The metaphysical poets made a last stand against the victorious army of smoothness; they sought to repenetrate the ancient mysteries of poetry. But the rich flowers of speech that fell so naturally from Elizabethan lips came cold from theirs. For this new[2] fashion in poetry[3] was all head, and no heart, and art with them lost its primary obligation and appeal. What they demanded in a writer was

> All point, all edge, all sharpness.

Shakespeare, says William Cartwright, the autocratic and well-received critic, has *vulgarised* drama. *His* best jest,

> I' the ladies questions and the fooles replies;
> Old fashioned wit,

is but 'old fashioned wit' that panders to the gallery.

It was a pedantic and self-conscious revival. There is no necessity to make "art" so "dull," says Carew[3]. Every conceit, painfully dragged to its duty, proclaims the labour of the artist. Cleveland works hard among the "fantastic" gang:

> Why doth my she Advowson fly
> Incumbency,

---

[1] Says Wither (in *Britain's Remembrancer*, 1628),
> Let no *fantastic* Reader now condemne
> Our *homely* Muse.

[2] See p. 207. [3] In *A Divine Love*.

he writes. But this machinery "knocks" terribly in serious poetry. It may be right for easy discursive comic poetry[1], for a roundabout essay, in prose or verse, but the manner must first be adjusted to the mood. Cartwright's lines on the effects of the great frost:

> Whiles waters thus are Pavements, firme as Stone,
> And without faith are each day walk'd upon,
> What Parables call'd folly heretofore,
> Were wisdome now, To build upon the Shore,

for example, are only poetically, not prosaically dull. But Cartwright, a typical metaphysical, lacked the "synoptic vision" of the imaginative poet; he simply "sat at ease" with fancy, and played his game of similes.

It is noteworthy in this connexion that Chalmers has traced the very great contemporary popularity of Cartwright to a certain "familiar easy humour" allied to his indubitable personal fascination. It may be admitted, and it is his most pleasing quality as a poet, that his verse does flow with remarkable ease over the rugged and often troublesome tenor of his thoughts.

Cartwright's critic in *The Retrospective Review* is very eulogistic; he notices a want of melody, but, he adds, though his imagery may not be powerful, there is "little conceit." It is difficult to support this opinion. A more sober criticism has been made by Ward in a note on Cartwright's play *The Ordinary*. "He overflowed," he

---

[1] In frankly comic verse Cartwright often scored a success, as in the poem *On Mr Stokes' Book of Vaulting*. Will Stokes is better than Daedalus,

> *He* us'd wax plumes, as Ovid sings,
> *Will* scorns to tamper with such things,
> He is a Daedalus without wings.

says, "with wit as distinguished from humour," and cites *A New Year's Gift to Bishop Duppa*[1] by way of example; here the

> Motion as in a Mill
> Is busie standing still,

and the phrases shuffle along in most awkward wise. A large fraction of the "conceits" in his poems are conventional and dead. It is distressing to hear the Prince of Wales described as

> The Eldest Tear of Balsam.

Here it is the ingenious poet, the "tutored poet" as he calls himself, who is writing. Again, he pleads for the renovation of the Christ Church buildings,

> But Ruines yet stand Ruines, as if none
> Durst be so good, *as first to cast a stone.*

He complains

> That now our windows may for Doctrine pass
> And we (as Paul, see Mysteries in a Glass.

Even the ancient laws

> If they had needed them, as now we do,
> Would have bestow'd the *Stone* for *Tables* too[2].

At the end of a good poem on the mortal illness of Mrs Sadleir, he writes

> We may Conclude her Feaver, without doubt
> Was but the Flaming Sword to keep Eve out.

"Eve out" was the highest tribute Cartwright could pay

[1] On p. 105.

[2] Yet *this* (good stuff again for comic poetry) was the kind particularly sought; this fact is proved in the note to the poem in question (p. 176). It was a "game," something akin to the "comic" pastoral elegies of which Goldsmith liked to make fun.

to any woman, and this indeed was the seventeenth
century "correct" estimate of women, flattering them to
heaven or debasing them very much to earth, but hardly
ever regarding them as natural and human beings. His
verses sometimes are so thronged with learned and curious
allusions that they become little else than what Burton
would call "laborious centos of divers writers." Perhaps
the poem on the birth of the Princess "Elizabeth[1]" is as
artificial as any, and the dead weights of its conceits
(references to the Elixir, the Golden Chain and the like)
drag down and drown all the struggling humankind-ness
in the poem.

We have said little of Cartwright's successes; the
reader will find many in this volume. His dainty addresses
To Chloe (pp. 63 and 66), and the finished *Tell me no more*
(p. 67), are graceful enough to whet the appetite of any
amateur of poetry[2]. To conclude, we may point to a good
passage on the virtue of Mrs Abigail Long:

> Something she had more Sacred, more Refin'd
> Than Vertue is, something above the Mind
> And low conceit of Man, something which Lame
> Expression cannot reach, which wants a Name
> 'Cause 'twas ne'r known before; which I express
> Fittest by leaving it unto a Guess[3].

[1] p. 78.
[2] If these are not enough, there are the octosyllabics *To Mr W. B.*,
which have a quaint flavour. Most of the lines *On a Gentlewoman's
Silk Hood* (p. 53) are good:

> Newly awak'd out of the Bud so shews
> The half seen, half hid, glory of the Rose,

for example.
[3] So in the lines on the Lady Newburgh (vide p. 129),

> where Art cannot express,
> It veyls and leaves the rest unto a Guess.

In Cartwright's poetry there is often some power and
some inspiration, but the pity of it is that it was so often
content with "lame expression," "low conceit" or the
mere "guess" of his "witty invention."

Cartwright's favourite metre was the heroic couplet,
but his best work was done either in stanzas or in lines of
four beats. His couplets are occasionally excellent; the
balance is well kept, for instance, in this:

> So by this Art Fancy shall Fortune Cross;
> And Lovers live by thinking on their Loss,

from the successful *Valediction*[1]. In paragraphing, Cartwright is usually either too stiff and pompous (as in the
Lines to Mr Thomas Killigrew[2]) or altogether too torrentially
fluent[3].

> A nest of Cupids hov'ring in one bright
> Cloud, did surprise my fancy, and my sight,

is far from the best example of the "new couplet," but it
employs a prosodic turn that would be successful but for
the sequence of the ugly "Cloud" and "did" mono-
syllables. Cartwright was too fond of monosyllabic words.
True, they are often the right thing for lyric. Herrick
achieved wonders in this kind, and the easy adaptability
of Cartwright's words to Lawes' airs no doubt strengthened
his popularity. But in heavy measures, lines like

> That when to take you Painters go about
> They be compell'd to leave some of you out

are very dull. The stiff iambic beat of the lines is frequently varied by notable trochaic openings—*Bid me not*

---

[1] p. 65.   [2] p. 121.

[3] Cf. *e.g.* the sentence, or portion of a sentence "Masses of Ivory"
to "cast into a Mould," lines 15-22 of the first poem (p. 1).

go, Tell me no more—where Cartwright was probably
original. But he uses little substitution;

> Low without creeping, high without loss of wings

is exceptional. Again, *-ation, -tion, -science,* at the end of
lines are invariably to be distended in pronunciation (in
the archaic Spenserian fashion) as in the lines

> Things may a while in the same order run
> As wheeles once turn'd continue Mótïón.

The couplet

> How his Beams meet, and joyn with Showers
> Tó awáke the sléeping Flówers

shows his formal use of the iambic measure. The reader
who at first gave only three beats to the latter line might
be excused. *Lesbia on her Sparrow*[1] is in almost uniformly
trochaic measure. *The Chambermaid's Posset*[2] is very
rough; certainly irregular, if not defective. Even sung
to a popular air, such lines could only jog.

We conclude with an echo of Chalmers' judgment;
Cartwright is well worth study. It is difficult indeed
after reading his work to realise his wonderful fame. He
was, let us remind ourselves, "the most noted poet, philosopher and orator of his time." His reputation was to
some extent fortuitous. He lived a full and active life—
the chances ever in his favour. He died an early and
pathetic death. But, as Lloyd suggests, there was something solid in Cartwright, a measure both of learning and
of poetic craftsmanship, and a power of interpreting the
spirit of his age, which promised, in the fullness of years,
a more lasting and glorious fruition. We can ill afford, in
any case, to pass him by. He commands respect both as

[1] p. 46.   [2] p. 50.

poet and as literary critic. For his utterances were de
livered to a wide and appreciative audience.

There can be no right appraisal of the seventeenth
century, of its literary notions and ideals, which does not
take William Cartwright, who was to it "so rare an example
of heroic worth," into consideration and account.

The following publications contain poems by Cartwright:

1630. *Britanniae Natalis*[1]. Oxon. No. 68. 1 Latin poem.
1631. *Ad...Iobannem Cirenbergium*[2]. Oxon. 1 Latin poem.
1633. *Pro Rege suo Soteria*[1]. Oxon. Nos. 50 and 94. Latin and
         English poems.
  „   *Solis Britannici P. rigaeum*[1]. Nos. 34 and 118. Latin and English
         poems. (Madan's index is here at fault; No. 34 *supra* is
         given as a third poem in the f llowing)
  „   *Vitis Carolinae Gemma Altera*[1]. Oxon. Nos. 27 and 106. Latin
         and English poems.
1635. *Amores Troili et Cresseidae*[1]. Oxon. 1 English poem.
1636. *Parentalia—Sir Rowland Cotton*[1]. Lond. 1 Latin poem.
  „   *Coronae Carolinae Quadratura*[2]. Oxon. Nos. 91 etc. Latin and
         English poems.
1637. *Flos Britannicus*[1]. Oxon. Nos. 23 and 89. Latin and English
         poems.
1638. *Death Repeal'd*[1]. Oxon. Nos. 3 and 27. Latin and English
         poems.
  „   *Charisteria...pro Maria*[1]. Oxon. Nos. 12 and 65. Latin and
         English poems.
  „   *Jonsonus Virbius*[1]. Lond. 1 English poem.
1639. (*The Royal Slave*)[1]. Oxon. 1st Edition.
1640. *Horti Carolini Rosa Altera*[1]. Oxon. No. 86. 1 English poem.
  „   *Honour and Virtue*[1]. Lond. 1 English poem.
  „   (*The Royal Slave*)[1]. Oxon. 2nd Edition.
1641. *Proteleia Anglo-Batava*[1]. Oxon. Nos. 19 and 49. Latin and
         English poems.

[1] In the British Museum.   [2] In the Bodleian.

1641. Stokes, *Art of Vaulting*[1]. Oxon. 1 English poem.

„[2] *To Philip, Earl of Pembroke*[3]. Oxon. 1 English poem (broad-side).

1642. *The Prisoners* and *Claracilla*[3]. By Thomas Killigrew. Latin and English poems.

1643. *Epibateria...Mariae*[3]. Oxon. Latin and English poems.

„ *Death of Sir B. Grenvill*[3]. Oxon.? 1643. 1 English poem (reprinted 1684).

„ *November*[3]. Oxon. Broadside (reprinted 1671); the two versions are both in the Bodleian (vide Note to the poem).

1647. Beaumont and Fletcher, *Comedies and Tragedies*[3]. Lond. 2 English poems.

1651. *Comedies, Tragi-Comedies with other Poems*[4]. Lond. By Mr William Cartwright. (Contains nearly all his English poems.) See above p. xxvii, and below p. xliv.

1652. *(An Offspring of Mercy)*[3]. Lond. A Passion Sermon.

1653, 1655. Henry Lawes, *Musical Ayres and Dialogues*[3]. (Several of Cartwright's poems are here set to music.)

„ *A Marrow of Compliments*[3].—A miscellany containing versions of Cartwright's poems.

1656. *Parnassus Biceps*[3] contains *To a Painter's Handsome Daughter, Wake, my Adonis*; *Hark, my Flora*; *On the Death of Lord Stafford*; *Upon Lady Paulet's Gift*.

„ *Sportive Wit*[5] contains the fine lyric *Hark, my Flora*, not included in the 1651 Edition. Other seventeenth-century miscellanies contain indifferent versions of the poems. See also

1744. Dodsley, *The Ordinary*, vol. x.

[1] Vide Note to "Stokes" poems, p. 183.

[2] *A declaration of the Kings...proceeding at Oxford, as it was related by a Student from thence* (Lond. 1642) purports to be the copy of a letter from W.C. in Oxford to T.H. in London. The first letter has certainly "the flourish and invention of a poet." The tract is probably a mere catchpenny forgery, but W.C. may very well mean our poet, and T.H. possibly Thomas Herbert (vide Note to the poem *To the Earl of Pembroke*, p. 200).

[3] In the British Museum.

[4] There are three copies in the British Museum. A portrait of the author by Lombert is a frontispiece to some editions.

[5] In the Bodleian.

Many of the poems may be found in MS. A collection of MS. poems was presented to Lady Pawlett in 1636, and the first of the poems is by Cartwright (MSS. Bodl. 22). An important notice of Cartwright appears in the *Chorus Vatum Anglicanorum* (British Museum, Addit. MSS. 24490). In the Catalogue of Bright's Library, No. 1042, *Secunda Vox Populi* is given as a poem of his. But see the note to the poem addressed to Herbert, Earl of Pembroke, p. 200.

A new edition of the Plays and Poems of William Cartwright was promised in 1779 "By the Author of the *Critical History of the English Stage.*" A notice of this appeared in *The Playhouse Pocket Companion* of that date, but the intention apparently was never carried out. (The dates assigned to Cartwright's plays in this notice are all wrong —*The Lady Errant*, 1657, *e.g.*) Again, Oldys mentions the "*Poemata Graeca et Latina a Gulielmo Cartwright e C.C.C. Oxon.*, promised to be printed very speedily by H. Moseley" at the end of Dr John Collop's *Poesis Rediviva*, 1656, but this, apparently, never appeared. Corser called attention also to Cartwright's Latin "compositions scattered abroad in various works." The Latin poems have been duly noted above.

BIBLIOGRAPHY

AUBREY, *Brief Lives*. Ed. Clarendon Press, 1, 148.
BELOE, *Anecdotes*, VI, 193; 310.
Bibl. Angl. Poet. No. 131.
Bibl. Heber. pt. IV, 275.
Biogr. Brit. vol. III, 287, Note by Kippis.
Biogr. Dram. vol. 1, 89.
Brit. Bibl. I, 206–7, 551.
BULLEN, A. II., Art. and Bibl. in *Dict. Nat. Biogr.*
Camb. Hist. Eng. Lit. vol. VI, VII, and Bibliographies.
CHALMERS, *English Poets*, vol. VI.
Clarendon State Papers (Domestic), 1636–7; 1640–1.
CORSER, *Collectanea*.
COURTHOPE, *Hist. Eng. Poet.* IV, 308, 384.
DIBDIN, *Libr. Comp.* II, 317.
ELLIS, *Specs. Early Engl. Poets*, III, 231.
EVELYN, *Diary*, ed. 1850, I, 421.
FOSTER, *Alumni Oxon.*
GERBER, *Sources of Cartwright's "Ordinary*[1]."
Gloucestershire, Harleian Soc. Publ. Visit. of 1623.
—— *Men and Armour for* 1608.
—— *Parish Registers*, ed. Phillimore.
—— *Victoria Hist. of*, 1907.
GRANGER, *Biog. Hist.* II, 367–8.
HEADLEY, *Beauties of Ancient Engl. Poets*, I, xxxi.
LANGBAINE, *Dramatick Poets* (Oldys MS. annots.).
LAWES, *Ayres and Dialogues*, Bks I–III.
LESSING, *Sämmtliche Werke*, XV, 230.
LLOYD, *Memoirs*, ed. 1668, pp. 422–5.

[1] In the Bodleian. A thesis, preceded by a Life of Cartwright, which, however, merely reproduces the account generally given. It aims to trace the Chaucerianisms in Cartwright's play.

MADAN, *Early Oxford Press.*
—— *Oxford Literature.*
MASSON, *Life of Milton.*
Monthly Review, XXVIII, 21.
Notes and Queries:
  (1st Series), I, 108, 151.
  (2nd Series) VIII, 207, 217, 423.
  (3rd Series), VIII, 287.
  (4th Series), II, 295; IV, 511.
  (5th Series), VIII, 447.
  (6th Series), XII, 168.
  (7th Series), VI, 187.
  (8th Series), XI, 47, 194, 253.
Playhouse Pocket Comp. Title, p. iv and 55.
Quarterly Review, XIII, 488; CLXXX, 121.
Retrosp. Review, IX, 160.
RUDDER, *Hist. of Gloucestershi...*
SANFORD, *Lives of Brit. Poets*, 1819.
WALKER, II, 64.
WARD, *English Dramatic Literature*, I, 510; II, 657; III, 137-140.
WELCH, *Alumni Westmonast.* ed. 1852, 100-1.
White Knights, 705.
WOOD, *Athenae*, ed. Bliss, III, 69-72, 161, 206, 454, 524; IV, 43, 418, 693.
—— *Fasti*, I, 468, 478; II, 56, 102.
—— *Hist. and Antiq.* II, 411, 447, 451; III, 508; App. 131.

Modern editions, often with excellent commentaries[1], of seventeenth-century writers, which have been consulted are not noticed above.

In the following pages, variant readings are given in footnotes; the originals for the text may be found in the *Notes*.

[1] Notably Grierson's edition of Donne.

ABBREVIATIONS, Etc.

Ed. 1651. The edition of Cartwright's work published in 1651 (vide p. xl). The copy of this edition belonging to the library of University College, London, has been chiefly used, but it has been collated with the three copies in the British Museum. The so-called Grenville copy (in the British Museum) contains parts of poems which have been deleted from the others by Royalist censors (vide pp. 202, 203).

The present volume does not profess to be a reproduction of the 1651 edition. Many of the poems contain variant readings from the MSS.

Ch. Text as in Chalmers, *English Poets*, vol. vi.

B.M. British Museum.

J.V. *Jonsonus Virbius*, London, 1638[1].

H. and V. *Honour and Virtue.* London, 1640[1].

A. and D. Lawes, *Ayres and Dialogues*, 1653-5[1].

M. of C. *A Marrow of Compliments*, 1653[1].

P.B. *Parnassus Biceps*, 1656[1].

[1] Vide pp. xxxix seq.

A PANEGYRIC TO THE MOST NOBLE LUCY
COUNTESSE OF CARLISLE

Madam,

    since Jewels by your self are worn,
Which can but darken, what they should adorn;
And that aspiring Incense still presumes
To cloud those Heavens towards which it fumes;
Permit the injury of these Rites, I pray,   5
Whose Darkness is increas'd by your full Day;
A day would make you Goddess did you wear,
As they of Old, a Quiver, or a Spear:
For you but want their Trifles, and dissent
Nothing in shape, but merely Ornament;   10
Your Limbs leave tracks of Light, still as you go;
Your Gate's Illumination, and for you
Only to move a step is to dispence
Brightness, and force, Splendor, and Influence;
Masses of Ivory blushing here and there   15
With Purple shedding, if compared, were
Blots only cast on Blots, resembling you
No more than Monograms rich Temples do,
For being your Organs would inform and be
Not Instruments but Acts in Others, We   20
What elsewhere is call'd Beauty, in You hold,
But so much Lustre, cast into a Mould;
Such a serene, soft, rigorous, pleasing, fierce,
Lovely, self-arm'd, naked, Majestickness,

Compos'd of friendly Contraries, do young   25
Poetique Princes shape, when they do long
To strik out Heroes from a Mortall Wombe,
And mint fair Conquerours for the Age to come.
But Beauty is not all that makes you so
Ador'd, by those who either see or know;   30
'Tis your proportion'd Soul, for who ere set
A common useless weed in Christall yet?
Or who with Pitch doth Amber Boxes fill?
Balsom and Odors there inhabit still;
As Jewels then have Inward Vertues, so   35
Proportion'd to that Outward Light they shew,
That, by their Lustre which appears, they bid
Us turn our sense to that which does lye hid;
So 'tis in you: For that Light which we find
Streams in your Eye, is Knowledge in your Mind; 40
That mixture of bright Colours in your Face,
Is equall Temperance in another place;
That vigour of your Limbs, appears within
True perfect Valour, if we look but in;
And that Proportion which doth each part fill,   45
Is but dispencing Justice in your will.
Thus you redeem us from our Errour, who
Thought it a Ladies fame, neither to know
Nor be her self known much; and would not grant
Them Reputation, unless Ignorant;   50
As Heroins heretofore did pass
With the same faith as Centaures and it was
A tenet, that as Women only were
Nature's digressions, who did thence appear
At best but fair mistakes, if they did do   55
Heroic Acts, th'were faults of Custome too:

But you who've gain'd the Apex of your kind,
Shew that there are no Sexes in the Mind,
Being so Candid, that we must confess
That Goodness is your Fashion, or your Dress.   60
That you, more truly Valourous, do support
Virtue by daring to be good at Court:
Who, beyond all Pretenders, are alone
So much a friend to't, that with it y'are One,
And when We Men, the weaker Vessels, do   65
Offend, we think we did it against you.
And can the thought be less, when that we see
Grace powrs forth Grace, Good Good, in one Pure, free
And following Stream, that we no more can tell,
What 'tis you shew, than what true tinctures dwel 70
Upon the Doves bright Neck, which are so One,
And Divers, that we think them all, and None.
And this is your quick Prudence, which Conveys
One Grace into another, that who saies
You now are Courteous, when you change the light, 75
Will say you're Just, and think it a new sight;
And this is your peculiar Art, we know
Others may do like Actions, but not so.
The Agents alter things, and what does come,
Powerfull from these, flows weaker far from some; 80
Thus the Sun's light makes Day, if it appear,
And casts true Lustre round the Hemisphere;
When if projected from the Moon, that light
Makes not a day, but only Colours Night;
But you we may still full, still perfect call, 85
As what's still great, is equall still in all.
    And from this Largeness of your Mind, you come
To some just wonder, Worship unto some,

Whiles you appear a Court, and are no less
Than a whole Presence, or throng'd glorious Press: 90
No one can ere mistake you. 'Tis alone
Your Lot, where e'r you come to be still known.
Your Powers its own witness: you appear
By some new Conquest, still that you are There.
But sure the Shafts your Vertues shoot, are tipt   95
With consecrated Gold, which too was dipt
In purer Nectar, for where e'r they do
Print Love, they print Joy, and Religion too;
Hence in your great endowments Church and Court
Find what t'admire; All wishes thus resort   100
To you as to their Center, and are then
Sent back, as Centers send back lines agen.

 Nor can we[1] say you learnt this hence, or thence,
That this you gain'd by Knowledge, this by Sence;
All is your own, and Native: for as pure   105
Fire lends itself to all, and will endure
Nothing from others; so what you impart
Comes not from Others Principles, or Art,
But is Ingenite all, and still your Owne,
Your self sufficing to your self alone.   110
Thus your Extraction is desert, to whom
Vertue, and Life by the same Gift did come.
Your Cradle's thus a Trophe, and with us
'Tis thought a Praise Confess'd to be born thus.
And though your Father's glorious Name will be   115
Full and Majestique in great History
For high designs, yet after Times will boast
You are his Chiefest Act, and fame him most.
Being then you're th'Elixar, whose least Grain

<hr />

[1] *you*, Chalmers.

Cast into any other, would maintain   120
All for true Worth, and make the piece Commence
Saint, Nymph, or Goddess, or what not from thence;
If when your Valorous Brother rules the Maine,
And makes the Flouds confess his powerful Raign,
You should but take the Aire by in your shell,   125
You would be thought Sea-born, and we might well
Conclude you such, but that your Deitie
Would have no winged Issue to set bye;
O had you Of-spring to resemble you,
As you have Vertues, then—But oh! I do   130
Complain of our misfortunes, not your Own,
For are bless'd Spirits, for less happy known
Because they have not receiv'd such a Fate
Of Imperfection, as to Procreate?
Eternall things supply themselves; so we   135
Think this your Mark of Immortalitie.

    I now, as those of old, who once had met
A Deity in a shape, did nothing set
By lower, and less formes, securely do
Neglect all else, and having once seen you,   140
Count others only Natures Pesantry.
And out of Reverence seeing will not see.

    Hail your own Riches then, and your own store,
Who thus rule others, but your self far more;
Hail your own Glass and Object, who alone   145
Deserve to see your Own Reflection;
Persist you still the Faction of all Vowes,
A shape that makes oft Perjuries, and allows
Even broken faith's a Pardon, whiles men do
Swear, and reclaim what they have sworn seeing you. 150
May you live long the Painters fault, and strife

Who, for their oft not drawing you to life,
Must when their Glass is almost run out, long
To purchase Absolution for the Wrong;
But poets, who dare still as much, and take   155
An equall License, the same Errours make,
I then put in with them, who as I do
Sue for Release, so I may claime it too.
For since your Worth, and Modesty is such
None will think this Enough, but You too Much.   160

ON THE IMPERFECTION OF CHRIST-CHURCH
BUILDINGS

Arise thou sacred heap, and shew a Frame
Perfect at last, and Glorious as thy Name:
Space, and Torn Majesty, as yet are all
Thou hast: we view they Cradle, as thy Fall.
    Our dwelling lyes half desert; The whole space   5
Unmeeted and unbounded, bears the face
Of the first Ages fields, and we, as they
That stand on hills, have prospect every way:
Like Theseus Sonne, curst by mistake, the frame
Scattred and Torn, both parts without a Name,   10
Which in a Landskip some mischance, not meant,
As dropping of the Spunge, would represent,
And (if no succour come) the Time's not far
When 'twill be thought no College, but a Quar.
Send then Amphion to these Thebes (O Fates)   15
W'have here as many Breaches though not gates.
When any Stranger comes, 'tis shewn by us,
As once the face was of Antigonus

With an half-visage onely: so that all
We boast is but a kitchen, or an Hall.   20
Men thence admire, but help not. 't hath the luck
Of Heathen places that were Thunder-strook,
To be ador'd, not touch't; though the Mind and will
Be in the Pale, the Purse is Pagan still:
Alas th'are Tower's that Thunder do provoke,   25
We ne'r had Height or[1] Glory for a Stroke;
Time, and King Henry too, did spare us; we
Stood in those dayes both Sythe, and Scepter-free;
Our Ruines then were licenc'd, and we were
Pass'd by untouch'd; that hand was open here.   30
Bless we our Throne then! That which did avoid
The fury of those times, seems yet destroy'd:
So this breath'd on by no full Influence
Hath hung e'r since unminded in suspence,
As doubtfull whether't should Escheated be   35
To Ruine, or Redeem'd to Majesty.
But great Intents stop seconds, and we owe
To Larger Wants, that Bounty is so slow.
A lordship here, like Curtius might be cast
Into one Hole, and yet not seen at last.   40
Two sacred things were thought (by judging souls)[2]
Beyond the Kingdomes Pow'r, Christchurch and Pauls,
Till, by a Light from Heaven shewn, the one
Did gain his second Renovation.
And some good Star ere long, we do not fear,   45
Will guide the wise to offer some gifts here.
But Ruines yet stand Ruines, as if none
Durst be so good, as *first to cast a stone.*
Alas we ask not Prodigies: wee'd boast

[1] *nor*, B.M. MS.   [2] *So that two sacred Things were thought,* ibid.

Had we but what is at one Horse-Race lost;⠀⠀⠀⠀50
Nor is our House, (as Nature in the fall
Is thought by some) void and bereft of all
But what's new giv'n: Unto our selves we owe
That Sculs are not our Churches Pavement now;
That that's made yet good way; that to his Cup⠀55
And Table Christ may come, and not ride up,
That no one stumbling fears a worse event,
Nor when he bows falls lower than he meant;
That now our windows may for Doctrine pass,
And we (as Paul) see Mysteries in a Glass,⠀⠀⠀60
That something elsewhere is perform'd, whereby
'Tis seen we can adorn, though not supply.
⠀⠀But if to all Great Buildings (as to Troy)
A God must needs be sent, and we enjoy
No help but Miracle; if so it stand⠀⠀⠀⠀⠀65
Decreed by Heav'n, that the same gracious Hand
That perfected our Statutes, must be sent
To finish Christ-Church too, we are Content;
Knowing that he who in the Mount did give
Those Laws, by which his People were to live,⠀70
If they had needed them, as now we do,
Would have bestow'd the *Stone* for *Tables* too.

A CONTINUATION OF THE SAME TO THE PRINCE OF WALES 1635[1]

But turn we hence to you, as some there be
Who in the Coppy wooe the Deity;
Who think then most successfull steps are trod

[1] vide Note on line 26.

When they approach the Image for the God.
Our King hath shewn his Bounty, Sir, in you,   5
By giving whom, h'hath giv'n us Buildings too.
For we see Harvests in a showre, and when
Heav'n drops a Dew, say it drops Flowers then,
Whiles all that blessed fatness doth not fall
To fill that Basket, or this Barn, but all.   10
We know y'have Vertues in you now which stand
Eager for Action, and expect Command;
Vertues now ripe, Train'd up, and Nurtur'd so
That they wait only when you'l bid them flow.
Indulge you then, Our Rising Sun, we may   15
Say your first Rayes broke here to make a Day:
For though the Light, when grown, pours fuller streams,
'Tis yet more precious in its Virgin Beams;
And though the third or fourth may do the Cure,
The Eldest Tear of Balsam's still most pure.   20
'Tis only then our Pride that we may dwell
As Vertues do in you, compleat and well;
That when a College finish'd, is the sport
And Pastime only of your yonger Court,
An Act, to which some could not well arive   25
After their fifty, done by you at five,
The late and Tardy Stock of Nephews may
Reading your Story, think you were born Gray;
This is the Thread weaves all our Hopes: for since
All better Vertues now are call'd the Prince   30
(As smaller Rivers lose their words, and beare
No name but Ocean when they come in there)
Thence we expect them, as these Streams we know
Can from no other Womb or Bosome flow;
Limne you our Venus then throughout, be she   35

Christned, some Part at least, your Deity;
That when to take you Painters go about,
They be compell'd to leave some of you out;
Whiles you shew something here that won't admit
Colours and shape, something that cannot fit.   40
Thus shall you nourish future Writers, who
May give Fame back those things you do bestow:
Where Merits too will be your work, and then
That Age will think you gave not stones, but Men.

ON HIS MAJESTIES RECOVERY FROM
THE SMALL POX, 1633

I doe confesse the overforward tongue
Of publike duty turnes into a wrong
And after Ages which could ne'er conceive
Our happy Charles so fraile as to receive
Such a disease, will know it by the Noyse   5
Which we have made, in shouting forth our joyes;
And our informing duty onely be
A well-meant spight, or loyall injury.
Let then the name be alter'd, let us say
They were small Starres fixt in a Milky way;   10
Or faithfull Turquoises, which Heaven sent
For a discovery, not a punishment;
To shew the ill, not make it; and to tell
By their paile looks, the Bearer was not well.
Let the disease forgotten be, but may   15
The joy returne, as yearely as the day.
Let there be¹ new Computes, let reckoning be

¹ by... Soteria, 1633.

Solemnely made from His Recovery:
Let not the Kingdomes Acts hereafter runne
From his (though happy) Coronation,   20
But from his Health, as in a better straine;
That plac'd Him in his Throne, this makes him Raigne.

.

TO THE KING ON HIS MAJESTIES RETURN
FROM SCOTLAND, 1633

We are a people now again, and may
Style our selves Subjects: your prolonged delay
Had almost made our jealousie engrosse
New feares, and rayse your absence into losse.
'Tis true the Kingdomes manners and the Lawe   5
Retain'd their wonted rigour; the same awe
And love still kept us loyale: but 'twas so
As Clocks once set in motion doe yet goe,
The hand being absent; or as when the quill
Ceaseth to strike, the string yet trembles still;   10
O count our sighs and feares! there shall not be
Againe such absence, though sure victorie
Would waite on every step, and would repay
A severall conquest for each severall day.
We doe not crown your welcome with a Name   15
Coyn'd from the Journey, nor shall soothing fame
Call't an adventure: Heretofore when rude
And haughty Power was known by solitude,
When all that Subjects felt of Majesty,
Was the oppressing yoke, and tyranny;   20
Then it had pass'd for valour, and had been

Thought Prowesse to have dar'd to have been seen;
And the approaching to a neighbour Region
No *Progress*[1], but an Expedition.
But here's no cause of a *Triumphall*[2] dance,   25
'Tis a returne, not a Deliverance:
Your pious Faith[3] secur'd your Throne, your Life
Was guard unto your Scepter: no rude strife
No violence there disturb'd the Pompe, unlesse
Their eager love, and Loyalty did presse   30
To see and know, whiles lawfull Majesty
Spread forth its Presence, and its Piety.
So hath the God, that lay hid in the voyce
Of his directing oracle, made choyce
To come in Person, and untouch't hath crown'd   35
The Supplicant with his Glory, not his sound.
Whiles that this Pompe was moving, whiles a fire
Shot out from you, did but provoke desire,
Not satisfie, how in loyalty did they
With an eternall solstice, or a day   40
That might make Nature stand, striving to bring
Ev'n by her wrong, more homage to the[4] King.
But may'st Thou dwell with us, Just Charles, and show
A Beame sometimes to them: so shall we owe
To constant light, they to Posterity   45
Shall boast of this, that they were seen by Thee.

[1] *prowesse* corrected to *Progress*, Ed. 1651.
[2] *triumphant*, Ed. 1651.
[3] *Raign*, S.B.P. and Ed. 1651, Ch. (corrected to *faith*).
[4] *a*, Ed. 1651, Ch.

TO THE QUEEN ON THE SAME OCCASION

We doe presume our duty to no eare
Will better sound than Yours, who most did feare.
We know your busie eye perus'd the Glasse,
And chid the lazy Sands as they did passe:
We know no houre stole by with silent[1] wing,   5
But heard one Sigh dispatch'd unto your King.
We know his faith too; how that other faces
Were viewed as Pictures onely; how their graces
Did in this onely call His eye, that seene
They might present some parcell of his Queene.   10
You were both maym'd, whiles sever'd; none could find
Whole Majesty: y'are perfect, when thus joyn'd.
We doe not thinke this Absence can adde more
Flames, but call forth those that lay hid before:
As when in thirsty flowers, a gentle dew   15
Awakes the sent which slept, not gives a new.
As for our joy, 'tis not a suddaine heat
Starts into Noyse; but 'tis as true, as great:
We will be try'd by Yours: For we dare strive
Here and acknowledge no Prerogative.   20
We then proclaime this Triumph be as bright,
And large to all, as was your Marriage-night
Cry we a second HYMEN then, and sing,
Whiles you receive the Husband, wee the King.

[1] *present*, Ed. 1651, Ch.

ON THE BIRTH OF THE DUKE OF YORK, 1633

The State is now past feare, and all that wee
Need wish besides is perpetuitee.
No gaudy traine of flames, no darkned Sunne,
No change inverting order did fore-runne
This Birth, no hurtlesse Natalitious fire   5
Playing about Him made the Nurse admire,
And prophecie. Forc'd[1] nature shewes these things
When Thraldome swels, when Bondmaids bring forth
    Kings.
And 'tis no favour: For Shee straight gives ore,
Paying these trifles, that She owe no more.   10
Here She's reserv'd, and quiet, as if Hee
Were Her Designe, Her Plot, Her Policie:
Here the enquiring busie Common-eye
Onely intent upon new Majestie,
Nere lookes for further wonders[2], this alone   15
Being sufficient, that Hee's silent showne.
What's Her intent, I know not: let it be
My pray'r, that She'll be modest, and that Hee
Have but the second honour, be still neere,
No imitation of the Father here.   20
Yet let him, like to him, make Pow'r as free
From blot or scandall, as from poverty;
Count Blood and Birth no parts, but something lent
Meerely for outward grace, and complement;
Get safety by good life, and raise defence   25
By better forces, Love, and conscience.
This likenesse[3] wee expect, the Nurse may finde

---

[1] *Fond*, Ed. 1651, Ch.   [2] *wonder*, Ed. 1651, Ch.
[3] *likewise*, Ed. 1651, Ch.

Something in Shape, wee'll looke unto his Minde.
The forehead, Eye, and lip, poore humble parts
Too shallow for resemblance, shew the arts   30
Of private guessings, action still hath beene
The Royall marke; those parts, which are not seene,
Present the Throne, and Scepter; and the right
Discoverie's made by judgement, not by sight.
I cannot to this cradle promise make   35
Of actions fit for growth. A strangled snake,
Kill'd before known, perhaps 'mongst heathen hath
Beene thought the deed, and valour of the Swath.
Farre be such Monsters hence! the Buckler here
Is not the cradle, nor the dart, and speare   40
The Infants Rattles: 'tis a Sonne of mirth,
Of peace and friendship, 't is a quiet birth.
Yet if hereafter unfil'd people shall
Call on his sword, and so provoke their fall,
Let him looke backe on that admired Name,   45
That Spirit of dispatch, that soule of fame,
His Grandsire Henry, tread his steps, in all
Be fully like to him, except his fall.
    Although in Royall births the Subjects lot
Be to enjoy what's by the Prince begot;   50
Yet fasten, CHARLES, fasten those eyes you owe
Unto a people, on this Sonne, to show
You can be tender too, in this one thing
Suffer the Father to depose the King.
See what delight your Queene takes to peruse   55
These[1] faire unspotted Volumes, when she views
In Him that glance, in Her that decent grace,
In this sweet innocence, in All the face

---

[1] *Those*, Ed. 1651, Ch.

Of both the Parents. May this blessing prove
A welcome trouble, puzzling equal love   60
How to dispense embraces, whiles that Shee
Strives to divide the Mother 'twixt all Three.

TO DR DUPPA, THEN DEAN OF CHRIST-CHURCH, AND TUTOR TO THE PRINCE OF WALES

Will you not stay then, and vouchsafe to be
Honour'd a little more Contractedly?
The Reverence here's as much, Though not the Presse[1];
Our Love as Tender, though the Tumult Less;
And your great Vertues in this narrow Sphere,   5
Though not so Bright, shine yet as strong as there;
As Sun Beames drawn into a point do flow
With greater force by being fettred so.
Things may awhile in the same Order run,
As wheels once turn'd continue Motion;   10
And we enjoy a Light, as when the Eye
O'th' World is set all Lustre doth not dye:
But yet this Course, this Light, will so appear,
As only to Convince you have been here.
He's Ours you ask (Great Soveraign) Ours, whom we 15
Will gladly ransome with a Subsidy;
Ask of us Lands, Our College, All; we do
Profer what's built, nay, what's intended too:
For he being Absent, 'tis an Heap, and we
Only a Number, no Society   20
Hard Rival! for we dare Contest, and use
Such Language, now w'have nothing left to lose.

[1] *Prease*, Ed. 1651, Ch.

Y'are only Ours, as some great Ship, that's gone
A Voyage i'th' Kings service, doth still run
Under the name o'th' Company: But we   25
Think it th' Indulgence of his Majesty
That y'are not whole engross'd, that yet you are
Permitted to be something that we dare
Call Ours, being honour'd to retain you thus,
That one Rule may direct the Prince, and us.   30
    Go then another Nature to him; go
A genius wisht by all, except the Foe:
Fashion those ductile manners, and inspire
That ample Breast with clean and Active fire;
That when his Limbs shall write him Man, His Deeds 35
May write him yours; That from those Richer seeds
Thus sprouting we dividedly may ow
The Son unto our King, the Prince to you.
'Tis in the Power of your great Influence,
What England shall be fifty harvests hence;   40
You'l do good to our Nephews now, and be
A Patron unto those you will not see;
Y'instruct a future Common-wealth, and give
Laws to those People, that as yet don't live.
We see him full already; There's no fear,   45
Of subtle poyson, for good Axiomes, here
All will be Health and Antidote, and one
Name will Combine State and Religion;
Heaven and we be look'd on with one Eye,
And the same Rules guide Faith and Policy: 50
The Court shall hence become a Church, and you,
In one, be Tutor to a People too.
He shall not now, like other Princes, hear
Some Morall Lecture when the Dinner's neer,

Learn nothing fresh and fasting, but upon   55
This or that Dish read an Instruction;
Hear Livy told, admire some Generals force
And Stratagem, twixt first and second Course;
Then cloze his Stomach with a Rule, and stay
'Mong Books perhaps to pass a Rainy day;   60
Or his charg'd Memory with a Maxime task
To take up time before a Tilt or Masque:
No, you will Dictate wholesome grounds, and sow
Seeds in his Mind, as pure as that is now;
Breath in your Thoughts, your Soul, make him the
      true   65
Resemblance of your worth, speak and live you:
That no old granted Sutour may still fear,
When't shall be one, to promise, and to swear.
That those huge Bulks, his Guard, may only be
Like the great Statues in the Gallery   70
For Ornament not use; not to Afright
Th'Approachers Boldness, but afford a sight,
Whiles he, defended by a better Art,
Shall have a stronger Guard in every Heart,
And carrying your Vertues to the Throne,   75
Find that his best defence, t'have need of none.
    May he come forth your work, and thence appear
Sacred and Pious, whom our Love may fear;
Discover you in all his Actions, be
'Bove Envy Great, Good above Flattery,   80
And by a perfect fulness of each part,
Banish from Court that Torment, and This Art.
    Go O my wishes with you: may they keep
Noise off, and make your Journey as your sleep,
Rather repose than Travell: May you meet   85

No rough way, but in these unequal feet,
Good Fates take Charge of you; and let this be
Your sole ill-luck, that Good is wisht by me.

TO THE SAME IMMEDIATELY AFTER THE PUBLICK ACT AT OXON. 1634

And now (most worthy Sir) I've time to shew
Some Parcell of that Duty that I ow,
Which like late fruit, grows Vigorous by delay,
Gaining a force more lasting by its stay.
Had I presented you with ought, whiles here,   5
'T had been to sacrifice,[1] the Priest not neer;
Forme rather than devotion, and a free
Expression of a Custome, not of me:
I was not then myself; Then not to err
Had been a trespass 'gainst the Miniver   10
For, when our Pumps are on, we do dispence
With every slip, nay, every Crime, but Sense:
And we're encouraged in't, the Statutes d't
Which bind some Men to shew they cann't dispute.
Suffer me, sir, to tell you that we do   15
Owe these few daies solemnity to you:
For had you not among our Gowns been seen
Enlivening all, Oxford had only been
A peopled Village. and our Act at best
A learned Wake, or Glorious shepheards feast: 20
Where (in my Judgement) the best thing to see
Had been Jerusalem or Nineveh,

---

[1] Comma given only in *Errata*, Ed. 1651.

Where, for true Exercise, none could surpass
The Puppets, and Great Britaines Looking Glass.
Nor are those Names unusuall; July here 25
Doth put forth all th'Inventions of the year:
Rare Works, and rarer Beasts do meet; we see
In the same street Africk and Germany
Trumpets 'gainst Trumpets blow, the Faction's much,
These cry the Monster—Masters, Those the Dutch: 30
All Arts find welcome, all men come to do
Their Tricks and slights; Juglers, and Curats too,
Curats that threaten Markets with their Looks,
Arm'd with two weapons, Knives and Table-books;
Men that do itch (when they have eate) to note 35
The chief distinction 'twixt the Sheep, and Goat;
That do no questions relish but what be
Bord'ring upon the Absolute Decree,
And then haste home, lest they should miss the lot
Of venting Reprobation, whiles 'tis hot. 40
But, above all Good sports, give me the sight
Of the Lay Exercise on Mondy night,
Where a Reserved stomach doth profess
A zeal-prepared Hunger, of no less
Than ten days laying up, where we may see 45
How they repaire, how ev'ry man comes Three.
Where, to the envy of our Townsmen, some
Men that themselves do victuall twice a year
At Christmas with their Landlords, and once here.
None praise the Act more, and say less; they do 50
Make all Wine good by drinking, all Beer too;
This was their Christian Freedom here: nay we,
Our selves too then, durst plead a Liberty:
We reform'd Nature, and awak'd the Night,

Making it spring as Glorious as the Light,　　55
That, like the Day did dawn and break forth here,
Though in a Lower, yet as bright a Sphere
Sleep was a thing unheard of, unless 'twere
At Sermon after Dinner, all wink'd there;
No brother then known by the rowling White,　　60
Ev'n they sate there as Children of the Night;
None come to see and to be seen; none heares,
My Lords fee-buck closeth bothe Eyes and Eares;
No Health did single, but our Chancellors pass,
Viscounts and Earls throng'd seven in a Glass;　　65
Manners and Language ne'r more free; some meant
Scarce one thing and did yet all Idioms vent;
Spoke Minshew in a Breath; the Inceptors wine
Made Latine Native: Gray Coats then spoke fine,
And thought that wiser Statute had done wrong　　70
T'allot us four years yet to learn the Tongue.
　　But Oxford, though throng'd with such People, was
A Court where e'r you only pleas'd to pass;
We reckon'd this your gift, and that this way
Part of the Progress, not your journey lay.　　75
　　I could relate you more, But that I fear
You'd find the Dreggs o'th' time surviving here;
And that gets some Excuse: Think then you see
Some Reliques of the Act move yet in me.

ON THE GREAT FROST, 1634

Shew me the[1] flames you brag of, you that be
Arm'd with those two fires, wine, and Poetry:
Y'are now benum'd spight of your Gods[2] and Verse;

---

[1] *your*, Malone MS.　　　　[2] *God*, ibid.

And may[1] your Metaphors for Prayers rehearse;
Whilst you that call'd Snow Fleece, and Feathers, doe 5
Wish for true Fleeces, and true Feathers too.
Waters have bound themselves, and cannot run,
Suff'ring what Xerxes fetters would have done;
Our Rivers are one Christall; Shoares are fit
Mirrours, being now, not like to Glass, but it: 10
Our Ships stand all as planted, wee may swear
They are not borne up only, but grow there.
Whiles waters thus are Pavements, firme as Stone,
And without faith are each day walk'd upon,
What Parables call'd folly heretofore, 15
Were wisdome now, To build upon the Shore.
There's[2] no one dines among us with washt hands,
Water's as scarce here, as in Africk Sands;
And we expect it not but from some God
Opening a fountain[3], or some Prophets Rod, 20
Who need not seek out where he may unlock
A stream, what e'r be strook would be true Rocke
When Heaven drops[4] some smaller Showers, our sense
Of Griefe's encreas'd, being but deluded thence;
For whiles we think those drops to entertaine, 25
They fall down Pearl, which half-way came down Rain.
Green-Lands Removall[5], now the poor man fears,
Seeing all waters frozen, but his Tears.
We suffer Day continnuall, and the Snow
Doth make our[6] Little Night become Noon now. 30
We hear of some Enchristal'd such as have
That which procur'd their death, become their Grave.
Bodies, that destitute of soul yet stood,

---

[1] *doe*, Mal. [2] *Here's*, ibid. [3] *some fountains*, ibid.
 dropt, ibid. [6] *Removing*, ibid. [8] *one*, ibid.

Dead, and not faln[1], drown'd, and without a Floud,
Nay we, who breath still, are almost as they,   35
And only may be stil'd a softer Clay;
We stand like Statues, as if Cast, and fit
For life, not having, but expecting it;
Each man's become the Stoick's wise one hence;
For can you look for[2] Passion, where's no Sense?   40
Which we have not, resolved to our first Stone,
Unless it be one Sense to feel w'have none.
Our very Smiths now work not, nay what's more,
Our Dutchmen[3] write but five hours and give o'r.
We dare provoke Fate now: we know what is   45
That last cold Death, only by suff'ring this.
All fires are Vestall now, and we as they,
Do in our Chimneys keep a lasting Day;
Boasting within doores this domestique Sun,
Adored too with our Religion.   50
We laugh at fire-briefs now, although they be
Commended to us by His Majesty;
And 'tis no Treason, for we cannot guess
Why we should pay them for their happiness
Each hand would be a *Scaevola's*: let *Rome*   55
Call that a pleasure henceforth, not a doom.
A Feaver is become a wish: we sit
And think fall'n Angels have one[4] Benefit,
Nor can the[5] thought be impious, when we see
Weather, that Bowker durst not Prophesie;   60
Such[6] as may give new Epochaes, and make
Another SINCE in his bold Almanack;
Weather may save his doom, and by his foe

---

[1] *fell*, Mal.   [2] *how can there be*, ibid.   [3] *Dutch*, ibid.
[4] *a*, ibid.   [5] *your*, ibid.   [6] *Weather*, ibid.

Be thought enough for him to undergo.
We now think Alabaster[1] true, and look 65
A sudden Trump should antedate his Book;
For whiles we suffer this, ought we not fear
The world shall not survive to a fourth year?
And sure we may conclude weak Nature old
And crazed now, being[2] shee's grown so cold. 70
But Frost's not all our Grief: we that so sore
Suffer its stay, fear its departure more:
For when that leaves us, which so long hath stood,
'Twill make a new accompt from th'second floud.

TO THE RIGHT VERTUOUS LADY ELIZABETH POWLET

UPON HER PRESENT TO THE UNIVERSITY OF OXON, BEING THE BIRTH, DEATH, RESSURECTION AND ASCENSION OF OUR SAVIOUR, WROUGHT BY HER SELFE IN NEEDLEWORKE

Could we judge here (most vertuous Madam) then
Your needle might receive praise from our[3] Pen:
But this our want bereaves it of that part,
Whiles to Admire and Thanke is all our Art.
  The Work deserves a Shrine, I should rehearse 5
Its Glories in a Story, not a Verse;
Colours are mixt so subt'ly, that thereby
The stealth[4] of Art both takes and cheates the Eye;

---

[1] *Allestree*, Mal.   [2] *when tha*, ibid.
[3] *the*, Ed. 1651, Ch. [4] *strength*, P.B.

At once a Thousand we can gaze upon,
But are deceiv'd by theire Transition;   10
What toucheth is the same; Beame takes from
    Beame.
The Next still like, yet diff'ring in the extreme:
Here runs This Track we see, Thither[1] That tends,
But cann't say here This rose, or there that ends.
Thus whiles they creep insensibly, wee doubt   15
Whether the one powres not the other out.
Faces so quick and lively, that wee may
Feare if wee turne our backs[2] they'l steale away.
Postures of Griefe so true, that wee may swear
Your artfull Fingers have wrought Passion there: 20
View we[3] the Manger and the Babe, wee thence
Believe the very Threads have Innocence;
Then on the Cross such Love, such Grief we find,
As 'twere a Transcript of our Saviours mind;
Each Parcell so expressive, and so fit,   25
That the whole seems not so much wrought, as writ.
'Tis Sacred Text all, we may quoat, and thence
Extract what may be press'd in our defence.

    Blest Mother of the Church, be in the list
Reckon'd from hence the Shee Evangelist: 30
Nor can the Style be Profanation, when
The Needle may Convert more than the Pen.
When Faith may Come by seeing, and each leafe
Rightly perus'd prove Gospell to the Deafe
Had not St.[4] Helen happ'ly found the Crosse,   35
By this your Work you had repar'd that Losse.

---

[1] *this tract thither we see*, P.B.

[2] *aside*, Ed. 1651, Ch.; *and*, Ed. 1651, Ch.

[3] *me* corrected to *we*, Ed. 1651.   [4] *that*, P.B.

Tell me not of Penelope, wee doe
See a web here more Chast, and Sacred too.
Where are ye now, O women, yee[1] that Sow
Temptations, labouring to expresse the Bow   40
And the Blind Archer, yee that rarely set,
To please your Loves, a Venus in a Nett?
Turn your skill hither: then we shall (no doubt)
See the Kings Daughter glorious too without.
  Women sew'd Idle[2] Fig leaves hithertoo,   45
  Eve's Nakedness is onlie[3] cloth'd by you.

TO MR. W. B. AT THE BIRTH OF HIS FIRST CHILD

Y'are now transcrib'd, and Publike View
Perusing finds the Coppy true,
Without Erratas new crept in,
Fully Complete and Genuine:
And nothing wanting can espy,   5
But only Bulk and quantity:
The Text in Letters small we see,
And the Arts in one Epitome.
O what pleasure do you take
To hear the Nurse discovery make,   10
How the Nose, the lip, the Eye,
The Forehead full of Majesty,
Shews the Father? how to this
The Mothers Beauty added is:

[1] *you,* Ed. 1651, Ch.
[2] *onely,* P.B.
[3] *truly,* Ed. 1651, Ch.

And after all with gentle Numbers   15
To wooe the Infant into Slumbers.
   And these delights he yields you now,
The Swath, and Cradle, this doth shew:
But hereafter when his force
Shall wield the Rattle, and the Horse;   20
When his ventring Tongue shall speak
All Synaloephoes, and shall break
This word short off, and make that two,
Pratling as Obligations do;
'Twill ravish the delighted Sense   25
To view these sports of Innocense,
And make the wisest dote upon
Such pretty Imperfection[1].
   These Hopefull Cradles promise such
Future Goodness, and so much,   30
That they prevent my Prayers, and I
Must wish but for formality.
   I wish Religion timely be
Taught him with his A.B.C.
I wish him Good and Constant Health,   35
His Fathers learning, but more wealth;
And that to use, not Hoard; a Purse
Open to bless, not shut to curse.
May he have many, and fast, friends,
Meaning Good-will, not private Ends,   40
Such as scorn to understand,
When they name Love, a peece of Land.
May the Swath and Whistle be
The hardest of his Bonds. May he
Have no sad Cares to break his sleep,   45

[1] *Imperfections*, Ed. 1651.

Nor other Cause, than now to weep.
May he ne'r live to be again
What he is now, a Child: May Pain
If it do visit, as a Guest
Only call in, not dare to rest.   50

FOR A YOUNG LORD TO HIS MISTRIS, WHO HAD TAUGHT HIM A SONG

Taught from your Artfull Strains, My Fair,
I've only liv'd e'r since by Air;
Whose Sounds do make me wish I were
Either all Voice, or else all Eare.
If Souls (as some say) Musick be   5
I've learnt from you there's one in me;
From you, whose Accents make us know
That sweeter Spheres move here below;
From you, whose limbs are so well met
That we may swear your Bodie's Set: 10
Whose Parts are with such Graces Crown'd,
That th'are that Musick without sound.
I had this Love perhaps before,
But you awak'd and made it more:
As when a gentle Evening Showre   15
Calls forth, and adds, Sent to the Flower;
Henceforth I'l think my Breath is due
No more to Nature, but to you.
Sing I to pleasure then, or Fame,
I'l know no Antheme, but your Name;   20
This shall joy Life, this sweeten Death:
You, that have taught, may claim, my Breath.

ON MR. STOKES HIS BOOK ON THE ART OF VAULTING

OR

In librum vere Cabalisticum de Ascensu Corporum gravium h.e. in Tractatu de Arte Saliendi editum a Guil. Stokes Almae Academiae Hipparcho, solo temporum horum Ephialte, Carmen desultorium

Reader, here is such a Booke,
Will make you leape before you look,
And shift, without being thought a Rooke.

The Author's Airy, light, and thin;
Whom no man saw e'r breake a Shin,   5
Or ever yet leap out of's Skin.

When e'er he strain'd at horse, or bell,
Tom Charles himself who came to smell
His faults, still swore 'twas clean and well.

His tricks are here in figures dimme,   10
Each line is heavier than his Limbe
And Shadows weighty are to him.

Were Dee alive, or Billingsley,
We shortly should each passage see
Demonstrated by A.B.C.   15

How they would vex their Mathematicks,
Their Ponderations, and their Staticks,
To shew the Art of these Volaticks?

Bee A the horse, and the man B:
Parts from the girdle upwards C,   20
And from the girdle downwards D.

If the parts D. proportion'd weigh
To the parts C. neither will sway,
But B. lye equall upon A.

Thus would his Horse and all his Vectures,   25
Reduc'd to figures, and to sectures,
Produce new Diagrams and Lectures.

And justly too, for the *Pomado*
And the most intricate Strapado
He'l do for naught in a Bravado.   30

The *Herculean Leape* he can with sleight,
And that twice fifty times a night,
To please the Ladys: *Will* is right.

The *Angelica* ne're put him to't,
Then for the *Pegasus*, hee'll doe't   35
And strike a Fountaine with his foot.

When he the *Stag-Leape* does, you'd sweare
The Stag himselfe, if he were there,
Would like the unwieldy Oxe appeare.

He'l fit his strength, if you desire,   40
Just as his horse, Lower or Higher,
And twist his Limbs like nealed wyer.

Had you, as I, but seen him once,
You'd swear that Nature for the nonce,
Had made his body without bones.   45

For Arms, sometimes hee'l hang[1] on one,
Sometimes on both, sometimes on none,
And like a Meteor hang alone.

---

[1] *lye*, Ed. 1651.

Let none henceforth our eares abuse,
How Daedalus scap'd the twining Stewes,   50
Alas that is but flying news.

He us'd wax plumes, as Ovid sings,
Will scorns to tamper with such things,
He is a Daedalus without wings.

Good faith, the Mewes had best look to't   55
Lest they go down, and Sheen to boot,
Will and his wooden horse will do't.

The Trojan Steed let Souldiers scan,
And praise th'Invention you that can,
Will puts 'em down both Horse and Man.   60

At once six Horses Theutobocchus
Leap'd o'r if Florus do not mock us,
'Twas well, but let him not provoke us;

For were the matter to be tri'd,
'Twere Gold to Silver on Wills side,   65
He'd quell that Theutobocchus Pride.

I'l say but this to end the brawle,
Let Theutobocchus in the fall
Cut Will's cross[1]-caper, and take all.

Then go thy ways, Brave Will, for one   70
By Jove 'tis thou must Leap, or none,
To pull bright honour from the Moon.

PHILIPPUS STOICUS E SOCIETATE
PORTAE BOREALIS OXON.

[1] *a,* Mal.

THE DREAME

I dream'd I saw my self lye dead,
  And that my Bed my Coffin grew;
Silence and Sleep this strange sight bred,
  But wak't, I found I liv'd anew.
Looking next Morn on your bright face,   5
  Mine Eyes bequeath'd mine Heart fresh pain,
A Dart rush'd in with every Grace,
  And so I kill'd my self again:
O Eyes, what shall distressed Lovers do,
If open you can kill, if shut you view.   10

LOVE INCONCEALABLE, Stig. Ital.

Who can hide fear? If't be uncover'd, light,
If cover'd, Smoake betraies it to the Sight:
Love is that fire, which still some sign affords,
If hid, th'are sighs; If open, they are words.

ON ONE WEEPING

Sawest thou not that liquid ball
Which from her tender eye did fall
Sure't'was no obedient drop
Taught at will to flow or stop
Such as the easy-tutour'd eye   5
Now keeps in, then lets flye.
I know the midst of mirth, that there
Are spongie eyes can squeeze a tearr.
I know there are of those that stand

At station and expect command   10
Streames traind to march in ranke and file
The foolish lovere to beguile.
But hers were true, and seeing there were
Of those before us did averre
The Soule was water may not I   15
Swear hers did glide out of her eye.
See upon the thirstye ground
Cleere and gentle, soft and round
Falls the dew and makes the earth
Travaile with a fruitfull birth.   20
So the bounty of the skie
Dropping fatness doth supplie
Th'impoverisht plant with life and feeds
The tender infancy of seedes.
O now the certaine cause I knowe   25
From whence the rose and Lilly grow
In her cheeke, the often showres
Which she weepes doth breede the flowers
Did the enamoured moisture steale
Downe to her lippe in hope to steale   30
That with a kisse? or would it faine
Salute her breast in hope to gaine
A wisht for entrance, there to sitt
With thoughts as innocent as it?
O tell mee what can wee deny   35
Petitioning humility?
O what suite can wee deterre
When your eye turns Oratour
A tear so true, so faire, so good
Might have stopt Deucalion's flood.   40
In this barren age of ours

Would out of waters and of showres
Call a god, as they before
Did heaven with Mars and Venus store.
Heere better might two gods arise   45
This from her cheekes, that from her eyes.

A SONG OF DALLIANCE

Heark, my Flora! Love doth call us
To that strife that must befal us.
He has rob'd his mother's Myrtles
And hath pull'd her downy Turtles.
See, our genial hosts are crown'd,   5
And our beds like billows rise:
Softer combat's nowhere found,
And who loses, wins the prize[1].

Let not dark nor shadows fright thee;
Thy limbs of lustre they will light thee.   10
Fear not any can surprise us,
Love himself doth now disguise us.
From thy waste thy girdle throw:
Night and darkness both dwell here:
Words or actions who can know,   15
Where there's neither eye nor ear?

Shew thy bosom and then hide it;
License touching and then chide it;
Give a grant and then forbear it,
Offer[2] something, and forswear it;   20
Ask where all our shame is gone[3];

---

[1] *Softer lists are nowhere found*
And the strife's itselfe's the prize, Parnassus Biceps.
Profer...

[3] *Ask where all my shame is gone*, ibid.

Call us wicked wanton men;
Do as turtles, kiss and groan;
Say "We ne'er shall meet again[1]."

I can hear thee curse, yet chase thee;   25
Drink thy tears, yet still embrace thee;
Easie riches is no treasure[2];
She that's willing spoils the pleasure.
Love bids learn the wrestlers' fight[3];
Pull and struggle whilst ye twine[4];   30
Let me use my force tonight,
The next conquest shall be thine.

PARCHMENT

Plain Shepherd's wear was only Gray,
And all Sheep then were cloath'd as they,
When Shepherds 'gan to write and think,
Some Sheep stole blackness from the Ink,
And we from thence found out the skill   5
To make their Parchment do so still.

FALSHOOD

Still do the Stars impart their Light
To those that travell in the Night;
Still Time runs on, nor doth the Hand
Or Shadow on the Diall stand;
The Streames still glide and constant are: 5

---

[1] *Say thou ne'er shalt joy againe*, Parnassus Biceps.
[2] *are no treasure*, ibid.   [3] *slight*, ibid.
[4] *when we twine*, ibid.

Only thy Mind
Untrue I find,
Which carelessly
Neglects to be
Like Stream, or Shadow, Hand, or Star.   10

Fool that I am; I do recall
My words, and swear thou'rt like them all:
Thou seemst like Stars to nourish fire,
But O how cold is thy desire?
And like the Hand upon the Brass,   15
        Thou point'st at me
        In mockery,
        If I come nigh,
        Shade-like thou'lt fly,
And as the Stream with Murmur pass.   20

Thrice didst thou vow, thrice didst thou swear,
Whisp'ring those Oaths into mine Eare,
And t'ween each one, as Seal of Bliss,
Didst interpose a sweeter kiss:
Alas that also came from Art,   25
        For it did smell
        So fresh and wel,
        That I presume
        'Twas thy Perfume
That made thee swear, and not thy Heart.   30

Tell me who taught thy subtile Eyes
To cheat true hearts with fallacies?
Who did instruct thy Sighs to Lie?
Who taught thy kisses Sophistry?
Believe't 'tis far from honest Rigour;   35

O how I loath
A tutor'd Oath!
I'l ne'r come nigh
A learned Sigh,
Nor credit Vows in Mood and Figure.   40

'Twas Venus to me whisper'd this,
Swear and embrace, protest and kiss,
Such Oaths and Vows are fickle things,
My wanton Son does lend them wings:
The kiss must stay, the Oath must fly: 45
        Heav'n is the Schoole
        That gives this Rule:
        I cann't prove true
        To that and you,
The Goddess is in fault, not I.   50

Who for any wrong would thus much do,
For my Revenge may something too;
She, O She make thee true to all,
Marry an Army, and then fall
Through scornfull Hatred and disdain: 55
        But mayst thou be
        Still false to me;
        For if thy mind
        Once more prove kind
Thou'lt swear thine Oathes all o'r again.   60

BEAUTY AND DENIALL

No, no, it cannot be; for who e'r set
A Blockhouse to defend a Garden yet?
Roses ne'r chide my boldness when I go

To crop their Blush; why should your Cheeks do so?
The Lillies ne'r deny their Silk to men; 5
Why should your Hands push off, and draw back then?
The Sun forbids me not his Heat; then why
Comes there to Earth an Edict from your Eye?
I smell Perfumes, and they ne'r think it sin;
Why should your Breath not let me take it in? 10
A Dragon kept the Golden Apples; true;
But must your Breasts be therefore kept so too?
All Fountains else flow freely, and ne'r shrink;
And must yours cheat my Thirst when I would drink?
Where Nature knows no prohibition, 15
Shall Art prove Anti-Nature, and make one?

But O we scorn the profer'd Lip and Face;
And angry Frowns sometimes add quicker Grace
Then quiet Beauty: 'tis that melting kiss
That truly doth distill immortall Bliss 20
Which the fierce struggling Youth by force at length
Doth make the purchase of his eager strength;
Which, from the rifled weeping Virgin scant
Snatch'd, proves a Conquest, rather than a Grant.

Beleeve't not: 'tis the Paradox of some One, 25
That in Old time did love an Amazon,
One of so stiff a Temper, that she might
Have call'd him Spouse upon the Marriage night;
Whose Flames consum'd him lest some one might be
Seduc'd hereafter by his Heresie: 30

That you are Fair and spotless, makes you prove
Fitter to fall a Sacrifice to Love:
Oh tow'rds his Altar then, vex not the Priest;
'Tis Ominous if the Sacrifice resist.
Who conquers still, and ransacks, we may say 35

Doth not Affect, but rather is in Pay.
But if there must be a reall Lists of Love,
And our Embracing a true wrestling prove,
Bare, and Annoint you then: for, if you'l do
As Wrestlers use, you must be naked too.   40

WOMEN

Give me a Girle (if one I needs must meet)
Or in her Nuptiall, or her winding sheet;
I know but two good Houres that women have,
One in the Bed, another in the Grave.
Thus of the whole Sex all I would desire,   5
Is to enjoy their Ashes, or their Fire.

TO CUPID

Thou, who[1] didst never see the Light,
Nor knowst the pleasure of the sight,
But alwaies[2] blinded, canst not say
Now it is Night, or now 't is Day,
So captivate her Sense, so blind her Eye,   5
That still she Love me, yet[3] she ne'r know why.

Thou who dost wound[4] us with such Art
We see no bloud drop from the heart,
And subtly Cruell leav'st no Sign
To tell the Blow or Hand was thine,   10
O gently gently wound my Fair, that shee
May thence[5] beleeve the wound did come from thee.

---

[1] *Cupid*, Lawes, Ed. 1655.   [2] *ever*, ibid.
[3] *though*, ibid.   [4] *that woundest*, ibid.
[5] *hence*, ibid.

A SIGH SENT TO HIS ABSENT LOVE

I sent a Sigh unto my Blest ones Eare,
Which lost it's way, and never did come there;
I hastened after, lest some other Fair
Should mildly entertain this travelling Aire:
Each flowry Garden I did search, for fear   5
It might mistake a Lilly for her Eare;
And having there took lodging, might still dwell
Hous'd in the Concave of a Christall Bell.
At last, one frosty morning I did spy
This subtile wand'rer journeying in the sky;   10
At sight of me it trembled, then drew neer,
Then grieving fell, and dropt into a Tear:
I bore it to my Saint, and pray'd her take
This new-born Of-spring for the Master's sake:
She took it, and prefer'd it to her Eare,   15
And now it hears each thing that's whisper'd there.
O how I envy Grief, when that I see
My sorrow makes a Gem, more blest than me!
Yet Little Pendant, Porter to the Eare,
Let not my Rivall have admittance there;   20
But if by chance a mild access he gain,
Upon her Lip inflict a gentle pain
Only for Admonition: So when she
Gives eare to him, at least Shee'l think of Me.

A COMPLAINT AGAINST CUPID

Venus, Redress a wrong that's done
By that yong Sprightful Boy, thy Son
He wounds, and then Laughs at the Sore

Hatred it self could[1] do no more.
If I pursue, Hee's small, and light,   5
Both seen at once, and out of sight:
If I do flie, Hee's Winged, and then,
At the first[2] step, I'm caught agen:
Lest one day thou thy self mayst suffer so,
Or clip the Wanton's wings, or break his Bow. 10

SADNESS

Whiles I this standing Lake,
Swath'd up with Ewe and Cypress Boughs,
    Do move by Sighs and Vows,
    Let Sadness only wake;
That whiles thick Darkness blots the Light,   5
My thoughts may cast another Night:
    In which double Shade
    By Heav'n, and Me made,
      O let me weep,
      And fall asleep,   10
    And forgotten fade.

Heark! from yond' hollow Tree
Sadly sing two Anchoret Owles,
    Whiles the Hermit Wolf howles,
    And all bewailing me,   15
The Raven hovers o'r my Bier,
The Bittern on a Reed I hear
    Pipes my Elegy
    And warns me to dye;
      Whiles from yond' Graves   20

---

[1] *can*, Ed. 1651.   [2] *third*, Ed. 1651, Ch.

My wrong'd Love craves
My sad Company.

Cease *Hylas*, cease thy call;
Such, O such was thy parting Groan,
    Breath'd out to me alone   25
    When thou disdain'd didst fall.
Loe thus unto thy silent Tomb,
In my sad winding sheet, I come.
    Creeping o'r dead Bones,
    And cold Marble Stones,   30
      That I may mourn
      Over thy Urn,
    And appease thy Groans.

CORINNA'S TOMB

Here fair Corinna buri'd lay,
Cloath'd and Lock'd up in silent Clay;
But neighb'ring Shepheards every morn
With constant tears bedew'd her Urn,
Untill with quickning moysture, she   5
At length grew up into this Tree:
Here now unhappy Lovers meet,
And changing Sighs (for so they greet)
Each one unto some conscious Bough
Relates this Oath, and tels that Vow,   10
Thinking that she with pittying sounds
Whispers soft Comfort to their Wounds:
When 'tis perhaps some wanton Wind,
That striving passage there to find,
Doth softly move the trembling leaves   15

Into a voice, and so deceives.
Hither sad Lutes they nightly bring,
And gently touch each querulous string,
Till that with soft harmonious numbers
They think th'have woo'd her into Slumbers   20
As if, the Grave having an Eare,
When dead things speak the dead should hear.
Here no sad Lover, though of Fame,
Is suff'red to engrave his Name,
Lest that the wounding Letters may   25
Make her thence fade, and pine away:
And so she withering through the pain
May sink into her Grave again.
O why did Fates the Groves uncare?
Why did they envy wood should hear?   30
Why, since Dodona's holy oake,
Have Trees been dumb, and never spoke;
Now Lovers wounds uncured lye
And they wax old in misery;
When, if true sense did quicken wood,   35
Perhaps shee'd sweat a Balsom floud,
And knowing what the world endures,
Would weep her moysture into cures.

TO THE MEMORY OF A SHIPWRACKT VIRGIN

Whether thy well-shap'd parts now scattred far
Asunder into Treasure parted are;
Whether thy Tresses, now to Amber grown,
Still cast a softer day where they are shewn;
Whether those Eyes be Diamonds now, or make   5

The Carefull Goddess of the Flouds mistake.
Chiding their lingring stay, as if they were
Stars that forgot t'ascend unto their Sphere;
Whether thy Lips do into Corall grow,
Making her wonder how't came red below;   10
Whether those Orders of thy Teeth, now sown
In severall Pearls, enrich each Channell one;
Whether thy gentle Breath in easie Gales
Now flies, and chastly fills the pregnant Sailes;
Or whether whole, turn'd Syren, thou dost joy   15
Only to sing, unwilling to destroy:
Or else a Nymph far fairer dost increase
The Virgin Train of the Nereides;
If that all Sense departed not with Breath,
And there is yet some Memory in Death,   20
Accept this labour, sacred to thy Fame,
Swelling with thee, made Poem by thy Name.
    Hearken, O winds (if that ye yet have Eares
Who were thus deaf unto my Fair ones Tears)
Fly with this Curse; may Cavernes you contain   25
Still struggling for Release, but still in vain.
    Listen O Flouds; black Night upon you dwell,
Thick Darkness still enwrap you; may you swell
Only with Grief; may ye to every thirst
Flow bitter still, and so of all be curst.   30
    And thou unfaithfull, ill-Compacted Pine,
That in her Nuptials didst refuse to shine,
Blaze in her Pile. Whiles thus her death I weep
Swim down my murmuring Lute; move thou the deep
Into soft numbers, as thou passest by,   35
And make her Fate become her Elegy.

TO A PAINTER'S HANDSOME DAUGHTER

Such are your Fathers Pictures, that we do
Beleeve they are not Counterfeits[1] but true;
So lively, and so fresh, that we may swear
Instead of draughts, He hath plac'd Creatures there;
People, not shadows; which in time will be   5
Not a dead Number, but a Colony:
Nay, more yet, some think they have skill and Arts,
That th'are well-Bred, and Pictures[2] of good Parts;
And you your Self, faire Julia, do disclose
Such Beauties, that you may seem one of those;   10
That having Motion gain'd at last[3], and sense,
Began to know it self, and stole out[4] thence.
Whiles thus his æmulous Art with Nature strives,
Some think H'hath none, Others he hath two Wives.
If you love none, fair Maid, but Look on all,   15
You then among his set of Pictures fall;
If that you look on all, and love all men,
The Pictures too will be your Sisters then,
For they as they have Life, so th'have this Fate
In the whole lump either to Love or Hate[5];   20
Your choice must shew you're of another Fleece,
And tell you are his Daughter, not his Piece:
All other proofs are vain; Go not about;
We two'l Embrace, and Love, and clear the doubt.
When you've brought forth your Like, the world will
    know   25
You are his Child; what Picture can do so?

[1] *counterfeit*, P.B.   [2] *They are well bred, pictures*, ibid.
[3] *least*, ibid.   [4] *from*, ibid.   [5] This couplet omitted in P.B.

LESBIA, ON HER SPARROW

Tell me not of Joy: there's none
Now my little Sparrow's gone;
    He, just as you
    Would toy and wooe,
He would chirp and flatter me,   5
He would hang the wing awhile,
Till at length he saw me smile,
Lord how sullen he would be?

He would catch a Crumb, and then
Sporting let it go agen,   10
    He from my Lip
    Would moysture sip,
He would from my Trencher feed,
Then would hop, and then would run,
And cry Philip when h'had done,   15
O whose heart can choose but bleed?

O how eager would he fight?
And ne'r hurt though he did bite:
    No Morn did pass
    But on my Glass   20
He would sit, and mark, and do
What I did, now ruffle all
His Feathers o'r, now let'em fall,
And then straightway sleek'em too.

Whence will Cupid get his Darts   25
Feather'd now to peirce our hearts?
    A wound he may,
    Not Love conveigh,

Now this faithfull Bird is gone,
O let Mournful Turtles joyn   30
With loving Red-breasts, and combine
To sing Dirges o'r his Stone.

THE GNAT

A Gnat mistaking her bright Eye,
For that which makes, and rules the Day,
Did in the Rayes disporting fly,
Wont in the Sun-Beams so to play.

Her Eye whose vigour all things draws,   5
Did suck this little Creature in,
As warmer Jet doth ravish straws,
And thence ev'n forc'd embraces win.

Inviting Heat stream'd in the Rayes,
But hungry fire work'd in the Eye;   10
Whose force this Captive Gnat obeys,
And doth through it her martyr dye.

The Wings went into Air; the Fire
Did turn the rest to Ashes there:
But ere death, struggling to retire,   15
She thence enforc'd an easie Teare.

Happy O Gnat though thus made nought,
We wretched Lovers suffer more,
Our Sonnets are thy Buzzings thought,
And we destroyed by what w'adore.   20

Perhaps would she but our deaths mourn,
We should revive to dye agen;
Thou gain'dst a Tear, but we have scorn;
She weeps for Flies, but Laughs at Men.

LOVE TEARES

Brag not a Golden Rain O Jove; we see
Cupid descends in Showers as well as thee.

A BILL OF FARE

Expect no strange, or puzzling Meat, no Pye
Built by Confusion, or Adultery
Of forced Nature; no mysterious dish
Requiring an Interpreter, no Fish
Found out by modern Luxury: Our Corse Board   5
Press'd with no spoyls of Elements, doth aford
Meat, like our Hunger, without Art, each Mess
Thus differing from it only, that 't is less.
Imprimis some Rice Porredge, sweet, and hot,
Three knobs of Sugar season the whole Pot.   10
Item, one pair of Eggs in a great dish,
So Ordered that they Cover all the Fish.
Item, one gaping Haddocks Head, which will
At least afright the Stomach, if not fill.
Item, one thing in Circles, which we take   15
Some for an Eele, but the Wiser for a Snake.
    We have not still the same, sometimes we may
Eat muddy Plaise, or Wheate; perhaps next day
Red, or White, Herrings, or an Apple Pye:
There's some variety in Misery.   20
    To this come Twenty Men, and though apace,
We bless these Gifts, the Meals as short as Grace.
Nor eat we yet in Tumult; but the Meat
Is broke in Order; Hunger here is neat;

Division, subdivision, yet two more   25
Members, and they divided, as before.
O what a fury would your Stomach feel
To see us vent our Logick on an Eele?
And in one Herring to revive the Art
Of Keckerman, and shew the Eleventh part?   30
Hunger in Armes is no great wonder, we
Suffer a Siedge without an Enemy.
     On Midlent-Sunday, when the Preacher told
The Prodigal's return; and did unfold
His Tender welcome, how the good old man   35
Sent for new Rayment, how the Servant ran
To kill the Fatling Calf, O how each Ear
List'ned unto him, greedy ev'n to hear
The bare Relation; how was every Eye
Fixt on the Pulpit; how did each man pry,   40
And watch, if, whiles he did this word dispence,
A Capon, or a Hen would fly out thence!
     Happy the Jews cry we, when Quailes came down
In dry and wholesome Showers, though from the frown
Of Heaven sent, though bought at such a Rate;   45
To perish full is not the worst of Fate;
We fear we shall dye Empty, and enforce
The Grave to take a Shaddow for a Corse:
For, if this Fasting hold, we do despair
Of life; all needs must vanish into Air;   50
Air, which now only feeds us, and so be
Exhal'd, like Vapours to Eternity.
W'are much refin'd already, that dull house
Of Clay (our Body) is Diaphanous;
And if the Doctor would but take the pains   55
To read upon us, Sinnews, Bones, Guts, Veines,

All would appear, and he might shew each one,
Without the help of a Dissection.
  In the aboundance of this want, you will
Wonder perhaps how I can use my Quill?   60
Troth I am like small Birds, which now in Spring,
When they have nought to eat do sit and Sing.

AT A DRY DINNER

Call for what wine you[1] please, which likes you best;
Some you must drink your Venison to digest.
Why rise you, Sir, so soon; you need not doubt,
He that I do invite sits my meal out;
Most true: But yet your Servants are gay men,   5
I'l but step home, and drink, and come agen.

THE CHAMBERMAID'S POSSET

My Ladies young Chaplain could never arive
  More than to four points, or thereabout:
He propos'd fifteen, but was gravell'd at five,
  My Lady stood up and still preach'd 'em out.

The Red-hatted Virtues in number but four,   5
  With Grief be remembred, for one was not:
The Habit's divine, not yet in our Power,
  Were Faith, Hope, and (Brethren) the third I ha' forgot.

Sir John was resolved to suffer a Drench,
  To punish[2] his Spirit with better Provision   10
A Posset was made by a Leviticall Wench,
  It was of the Chambermaid's own Composition.

      [1] *Your*, Ed. 1651.   [2] *furnish?*

The Milk it came hot from an Orthodox Cow
   Ne'r rid by the Pope, nor yet the Pope's Bull;
The heat of Zeal Boyled it, God knows how: 15
   'Twas the Milk of the Word; Believe it who will.

The Ingredients were divers, and most of them new,
   No Virtue was judg'd in an Antient thing;
n the Garden of Leyden some part of them grew,
   And some did our own Universities bring.   20

mprimis two handfulls of long Digressions,
   Well squeezed and press'd at Amsterdam,
They cured Buchanan's dangerous Passions,
   Each Grocer's Shop now will afford you the same.

Two ounces of Calvinisme not yet refin'd,   25
   By the better Physicians not thought to be good;
But t'was with the Seal of a Conventicle sign'd,
   And approv'd by the Simpling Brotherhood.

One Quarter of Practicall Piety next,
   With an Ounce and a half of Histrio-mastix,   30
Three Sponfulls of T.C.'s confuted Text,
   Whose close noated Ghost hath long since past Styx.

Next *Stript Whipt Abuses* were cast in the Pot,
   With the worm eaten Motto not now in fashion,
All these in the mouth are wondrous hot,   35
   But approvedly cold in operation.

Next *Clever* and *Doddisme* both mixed and fine,
   With five or six scruples of Conscience Cases,
Three Drams of Geneva's strict Discipline,
   All steept in the sweat of the silenc'd faces.   40

One Handfull of Doctrines, and Uses, or more,
  With the utmost Branch of the fifteenth point,
Then Duties enjoyn'd and Motives good store,
  All boyl'd to a Spoonfull, though from a siz'd Pint.

These all have astringent and hard qualities,   45
  And for notable Binders received be,
To avoid the Costiveness thence might arise,
  She allay'd them with Christian Liberty.

The Crumbs of Comfort did thicken the Mess,
  'Twas turn'd by the frown of a soure fac'd Brother, 50
But that you will say converts wickedness,
  'Twill serve for the one as well as the Other.

An Ell-London measure of tedious Grace,
  Was at the same time Conceiv'd, and said,
'Twas eat with a spoon defil'd with no face,   55
  Nor the Imag'ry of an Apostles head.

Sir John after this could have stood down the Sun,
  Dividing the Pulpit and Text with one Fist,
The Glass was Compell'd still Rubbers to run,
  And he counted the Fift Evangelist.   60

The Pig that for haste, much like a Devout
  Entranced Brother, was wont to come in
With white staring Eyes, not quite roasted out,
  Came now in a Black Persecution skinn.

Stale Mistris Priscilla her Apron-strings straite   65
  Let down for a Line just after his Cure:
Sir John did not nibble, but pouch'd the deceit:
  An Advouzon did bait him to make all sure.

ON A GENTLEWOMAN'S SILK HOOD[1]

Is there a Sanctity[2] in Love begun
That every woman veils and turns Lay-Nun.
Alas your guilt appears still through the dresse;
You doe not so much cover as confess:
To me 'tis a memoriall; I[3] begin   5
Forthwith to think on Venus and the Ginne,
Discovering in these Veyls, so subtly set
At least her upper parts caught in the[4] Net.
Tell me who taught you to give so much light
As may[5] entice, not satisfie the Sight,   10
Betraying what may[5] cause us to admire,
And kindle only, but not quench desire?
Among your other[6] subtilties, 'tis one
That you see all, and yet are seen of none;
'Tis the Dark Lanthorn to the face; O then   15
May we not think[7] there's Treason against Men
Whiles thus you only do expose the Lips?
'Tis but a fair and wantonner Eclipse
Mean't how you will, at once to shew, and hide
At best is but the Modesty of Pride;   20
Either unveil you then, or veil quite o'r
Beauty deserves not so much foulness more.
　　But I[8] prophane, like one whose strange[9] desires
Bring to Love's altar foul and drossie Fires:
Sink O those Words t'your Cradles[10]; for I know, 25

---

[1] *Gentlewomen's Black hoods*, B.M. MS.　　　[2] *chastity*, Mal.
[3] *to*, ibid.　　　[4] *a*, ibid.　　　[5] *will*, ibid.
[6] *other* is omitted ibid.　　　[7] *I may conclude*, ibid.
[8] *I*, omitted ibid.　　　[9] *strong*, ibid.
[10] *your Cradles*, omitted ibid.

Mixt[1] as you are, your Birth came from below:
My fancy's now all hallow'd, and[2] I find
Pure Vestals in my Thoughts, Priests in my mind.
    So Love[3] appear'd, when, breaking out his way
From the dark Chaos, he first shed[4] the Day;   30
Newly awak'd out of the Bud[5] so shews
The half seen, half hid, glory of the Rose,
As you do through your[6] Veyls; and I may swear,
Viewing you so, that Beauty doth Bud there.
So Truth lay[7] under Fables, that the Eye   35
Might Reverence the Mystery, not descry;
Light being so proportion'd that no more
Was seen, but what might Cause 'em to adore:
Thus is your[8] Dress so Ord'red, so Contriv'd.
As 'tis but only Poetry Reviv'd.   40
Such doubtful Light had Sacred Groves[8], where Rods
And Twigs, at last did Shoot up into Gods[9];
Where then a Shade darkneth the Beauteous Face
May not I[10] pay a Reverence to the place?
So under-water glimmering Stars appear,   45
As those (but nearer Stars) your Eyes do here.
So Deities darkned sit, that we may find
A better way to see them in our Mind.
No bold Ixion then be here allow'd
When Juno dares her self be in the Cloud.   50
Methinks the first Age comes again, and we
See a Retrivall of Simplicity;

---

[1] *Foule,* Mal.
[2] *and,* omitted ibid.
[3] *Jove...breaking forth,* ibid.
[4] *shewd,* ibid.
[5] *bed,* ibid.   [6] *the,* ibid.
[7] *layes,* ibid.
[8] *This is the,* ibid.
[9] defective ibid.
[10] *Shall I not,* ibid.

Thus looks the Country Virgin, whose brown hue
Hoods her, and makes her shew even[1] veil'd as you.
Blest Mean, that Checks our Hope, and spurs our Fear, 55
Whiles all doth not lye hid, nor all appear:
O fear ye no Assaults[2] from Bolder men;
When they assaile be this your Armour then.
A Silken Helmet may defend those Parts
Where softer kisses are the only Darts. 60

A DREAM BROKE

As Nilus sudden Ebbing, here
Doth leave a scale, and a scale there,
And somewhere else perhaps a Fin,
Which by his stay had Fishes been:
So Dreams, which overflowing be, 5
Departing leave Half-things, which we
For their Imperfectness can call
But Joyes i'th' Fin, or in the Scale.
If when her Teares I haste to kiss,
They dry up, and deceive my Bliss, 10
May not I say the Waters sink,
And cheat my Thirst when I would drink?
If when her Breasts I go to press,
Instead of them I grasp her Dress,
May not I say the Apples then 15
Are set down, and snatch'd up agen?
Sleep was not thus Death's Brother meant;
'Twas made an Ease, no Punishment.
As then that's finish'd by the Sun,

---

[1] *looke as*, Mal.   [2] *not Assault*, ibid.

Which Nile did only leave begun,   20
My Fancy shall run o'r Sleeps Themes,
And so make up the Web of Dreams:
In vain sweet shades, ye do Contest:
Awak'd how e'r I'l think the rest.

LOVES DARTS

Where is that Learned wretch that knows
What are those Darts the Veyl'd God throws?
O let him tell me ere I dye
When 'twas he saw or heard them fly;
    Whether the sparrows Plumes, or Doves   5
    Wing them for various Loves;
    And whether Gold, or Lead,
    Quicken, or dull the head:
I will anoint and keep them warm,
And make the weapons heale the Harm.   10

Fond that I am to aske! who ere
Did yet see thought? or Silence hear?
Safe from the search of humane Eye
These Arrows (as their waies are) flie:
    The Flights of Angels part   15
    Not Aire with so much Art;
    And snows on Streams, we may
    Say, Louder fall than they;
So hopeless I must now endure,
And neither know the Shaft nor Cure.   20

A sudden fire of Blushes shed
To dye white paths with hasty Red;

A Glance's Lightning swiftly thrown,
Or from a true or seeming frown;
  A subt'le taking smile   25
  From Passion, or from Guile;
  The Spirit, Life, and Grace
  Of motion, Limbs, and Face;
These Misconceits entitles Darts,
And Tears the bleedings of our hearts.   30

But as the Feathers in the Wing,
Unblemish'd are and no Wounds bring,
And harmless Twigs no Bloodshed know,
Till Art doth fit them for the Bow;
  So Lights of flowing Graces   35
  Sparkling in severall places,
  Only adorn the Parts,
  Till we that make them Darts;
Themselves are only Twigs and Quils:
We give them Shape, and force for Ills.   40

Beautie's our Grief, but in the Ore,
We Mint, and Stamp, and then adore;
Like Heathen we the Image Crown,
And undiscreetly then fall down:
  Those Graces all were meant   45
  Our Joy, not Discontent;
  But with untaught desires
  We turn those Lights to Fires.
Thus Natures Healing Herbs we take,
And out of Cures do Poysons make.   50

PARTHENIA FOR HER SLAIN ARGALUS

See thy Parthenia stands
Here to receive thy last Commands.
Say quickly, say, for fear
Grief ere thou speaks, make me not hear.
Alas, as well I may   5
Call to Flowers wither'd Yesterday.
His Beauties, O th'are gone;
His thousand Graces none.
This O ye Gods, is this the due
Ye pay to Men more just than you?   10
O dye Parthenia, Nothing now remains
Of all thy Argalus, but his Wounds and Stains.

Too late, I now recall,
The Gods foretold me this thy fall;
I grasp'd thee in my Dream,   15
And loe thou meltd'st into a Stream;
But when They will surprise,
They shew the Fate, and blind the Eyes.
Which wound shall I first kiss?
Here? there? or that? or this?   20
Why gave he not the like to me,
That wound by wound might answer'd be?
We would have joyntly bled, by Griefs ally'd,
And drank each other's Soul, and so have dy'd.

In silent Groves below   25
Thy bleeding wounds thou now dost shew;
And there perhaps to Fame
Deliver'st up Parthenia's Name;
Nor do thy Loves abate.

O Gods! O Stars! O Death! O Fate! 30
  But thy Proud Spoyler here
  Doth thy snatch'd Glories wear;
  And big with undeserv'd success
  Swels up his Acts, and thinks Fame less;
And counts my Groans not worthy of Relief, 35
O Hate! O Anger! O Revenge! O Grief!

  Parthenia then shall live,
And something to thy Story give.
  Revenge inflame my Breast
  To send thy wand'ring Spirit rest 40
  By our fast Tye, our Trust,
Our one Mind, our one Faith I must:
  By my past Hopes and Fears,
  My Passions and my Tears;
  By these thy wounds (my wounds) I vow, 45
  And by thy Ghost, my Griefe's God now,
I'l not revoke a Thought. Or to thy Tomb
My Off'ring He, or I his Crime will come.

ARIADNE DESERTED BY THESEUS, AS SHE SITS UPON A ROCK IN THE ISLAND NAXOS, THUS COMPLAINS

Theseus! O Theseus heark! but yet in vain
  Alas deserted I complain,
It was some neighbouring Rock, more soft than he,
  Whose hollow Bowels pittied me,
And beating back that false, and Cruell Name, 5
  Did Comfort and revenge my flame.

Then faithless whither wilt thou fly?
Stones dare not harbour Cruelty.

Tell me you Gods who e'r you are,
Why, O why made you him so fair?   10
    And tell me, Wretch, why thou
    Madst not thy self more true?
Beauty from him may Copies take,
And more Majestique Heroes make,
    And falshood learn a wile,   15
    From him too, to beguile.
      Restore my Clew
      'Tis here most due,
For 'tis a Labyrinth[1] of more subtile Art,
To have so fair a Face, so foul a Heart.   20

The Ravenous Vulture tear his Breast,
The rowling Stone disturb his rest,
      Let him next feel
      Ixion's wheel,
And add one Fable more   25
To cursing Poets store;
And then—yet rather let him live, and twine
His Woof of daies, with some thred stolen from mine;
    But if you'l torture him, how e'r,
    Torture my Heart, you'l find him there.   30

        'Till my Eyes drank up his,
          And his drank mine,
        I ne'r thought Souls might kiss,
          And Spirits joyn:
          Pictures till then   35

[1] *Lab'rinth*, Lawes, Ed. 1655.

Took me as much as Men,
Nature and Art
Moving alike my heart,
But his fair Visage made me find
Pleasures and Fears,   40
Hopes, Sighs, and Tears,
As severall seasons of the Mind.

Should thine Eye, Venus, on his dwell,
Thou wouldst invite him to thy Shell,
And Caught by that live Jet   45
Venture the second Net,
And after all thy dangers, faithless he
Shouldst thou but slumber, would forsake ev'n thee.

The Streemes so Court the yeelding Banks,
And gliding thence ne'r pay their thanks;   50
The winds so wooe the Flow'rs,
Whisp'ring among fresh Bow'rs,
And having rob'd them of their smels,
Fly thence perfum'd to other Cels.
This is familiar Hate to Smile and kill,   55
Though nothing please thee yet my Ruine will.
Death hover, hover o'r me then,
Waves let your Christall Womb
Be both my Fate, and Tomb,
I'l sooner trust the Sea, than Men.   60

Yet for revenge to Heaven I'l call
And breath one Curse before I fall,
Proud of two Conquests Minotaure, and Me,
That by thy Faith, This by thy Perjury,
Mayst thou forget to Wing thy Ships with White, 65
That the Black Sayl may to the longing sight

Of thy Gray Father, tell thy Fate, and He
Bequeath the Sea his Name, falling like me.
Nature and Love thus brand thee, whiles I dye
'Cause thou forsak'st, Ægeus 'cause thou drawest[1] nigh. 70

And yet O Nymphs below who sit,
In whose swift Flouds his Vows he writ;
Snatch a sharp Diamond from the[2] richer Mines,
And in some Mirrour grave these sadder Lines,
Which let some God Convey   75
To him, that so he may
In that both read at once, and see
Those Looks that Caus'd my destiny.
In Thetis Arms, I Ariadne sleep,
Drown'd first by my own Tears, then in the deep;   80
Twice banished, First by Love, and then by Hate,
The life that I preserv'd became my Fate;
Who leaving all, was by him left alone
That from a Monster freed himself prov'd one.

That[3] then I——But look! O mine Eyes   85
Be now true Spies,
Yonder, Yonder,
Comes my Dear.
Now my wonder,
Once my fear,   90
See Satyrs dance along
In a confused Throng,
Whiles Horns and Pipes rude noise
Do mad their lusty Joyes,
Roses his forehead Crown,   95

---

[1] *draw'st*, Lawes, Ed. 1655.   [2] *your*, ibid.
[3] *Thus*, ibid.

And that recrowns the Flow'rs,
 Where he walks up and down
He makes the desarts Bow'rs,
 The Ivy, and the Grape
 Hide, not adorn his Shape.   100
And Green Leaves Cloath his waving Rod.
'Tis either Theseus, or some God.

NO DRAWING OF VALENTINES

Cast not in Chloe's Name among
The common undistinguish'd Throng,
 I'l neither so advance
 The foolish Raign of Chance,
 Nor so depress the Throne   5
 Whereon Love sits alone:
If I must serve my Passions, I'l not owe
Them to my fortune; ere I love, I'l know.

Tell me what God lurks in the Lap
To make that Councell, we call Hap? 10
 What power conveighs the name?
 Who to it adds the Flame!
 Can he raise mutuall fires,
 And answering desires?
None can assure me that I shall approve 15
Her whom I draw, or draw her whom I love.

No longer then this Feast abuse,
You choose and like, I like and choose;
 My flame is try'd and Just.
 Yours taken up on trust.   20

Hail thus blest Valentine,
And may my Chloe shine.
To me and none but me, as I believe
We ought to make the whole year but thy Eve.

TO LYDIA WHOM MEN OBSERV'D TO MAKE
TOO MUCH OF ME

I told you Lydia how't would be,
Though Love be blind, his Priests can see;
Your Wisdom that doth rule the wise,
And Conquers more than your Black Eyes,
That like a Planet doth dispense,   5
And Govern by its Influence
(Though to all else discreet you be)
Is blemish'd 'cause y'are fond of me.

Your manners like a Fortress Bar
The Rough Approach of Men of War;   10
The King's and Prince's Servants you
Do use as they their Scrivenors do;
The learned Gown, the City Ruffe,
Your Husband too, scurvy enough;
But still with me you meet and Close,   15
As if that I were King of those.

You say, you ought how e'er to do
The same thing still; I say so too;
Let Tongues be free, speak what they will,
Say our Love's loud, but let's love still.   20
I hate a secret stifled flame,
Let yours and mine have Voice, and Name;
Who Censure what twixt us they see
Condemn not you, but envy me.

Go bid the eager flame Congeal   25
To sober ice, Bid the Sun steal
The Temper of the frozen Zone
Till Christall say that Cold's its own,
Bid Jove himself, whiles the grave State
Of Heaven doth our Lots debate,   30
But think of Leda, and be wise
And bid Love have equall Eyes.

View others Lydia as you would
View Pictures, I'l be flesh and bloud;
Fondness, like Beauty that's admir'd,   35
At once is Censur'd and desir'd;
And they that do it will Confess,
Your Soul in this doth but digress:
But when you thus in Passions rise,
Y'are fond to them, to me y'are wise.   40

A VALEDICTION:

Bid me not go where neither Suns nor Show'rs
    Do make or Cherish Flow'rs;
Where discontented things in sadness lye,
    And Nature grieves as I;
When I am parted from those Eyes,   5
From which my better day doth rise,
    Though some propitious Pow'r
    Should plant me in a Bow'r,
Where amongst happy Lovers I might see
    How Showers and Sun-Beames bring   10
    One everlasting Spring,
Nor would those fall, nor these shine forth to me;

Nature her Selfe to him is lost,
Who loseth her he honours most.
Then Fairest to my parting view display   15
    Your Graces all in one full day;
Whose blessed Shapes I'l snatch and keep, till when
    I do return and view agen:
So by this Art Fancy shall Fortune Cross;
And Lovers live by thinking on. their Loss.   20

TO CHLOE, WHO WISH'D HER SELF
YOUNG ENOUGH FOR ME

Chloe, why wish you that your years
    Would backward run, till they meet mine,
That perfect Likeness, which endears
    Things unto things, might us Combine?
Our ages so in date agree,   5
That Twins do differ more than we.

There are two Births, the one when Light
    First strikes the new awak'ned sense;
The Other when two Souls unite;
    And we must count our life from thence: 10
When you lov'd me, and I lov'd you,
Then both of us were born anew.

Love then to us did new Souls give,
    And in those Souls did plant new pow'rs;
Since when another life we live,   15
    The Breath we breathe is his, not ours;
Love makes those young, whom Age doth Chill,
And whom he finds young, keeps young still.

Love, like that Angell that shall call
   Our bodies from the silent Grave,   20
Unto one Age doth raise us all,
   None too much, none too little have
Nay that the difference may be none,
He makes two not alike, but One.

And now since you and I are such,   25
   Tell me what's yours, and what is mine?
Our Eyes, our Ears, our Taste, Smell, Touch,
   Do (like our Souls) in one Combine;
So by this, I as well may be
Too old for you, as you for me.   30

NO PLATONIQUE LOVE

Tell me no more of minds embracing minds,
   And hearts exchang'd for hearts;
That Spirits Spirits meet, as Winds do Winds,
   And mix their subt'lest parts;
That two unbodi'd Essences may kiss,   5
And then like Angels, twist and feel one Bliss.

I was that silly thing that once was wrought
   To practice this thin Love;
I climb'd from Sex to Soul, from Soul to Thought;
   But thinking there to move,   10
Headlong, I rowl'd from Thought to Soul, and then
From Soul I lighted at the Sex agen.

As some strict down-look'd men pretend to fast
   Who yet in Closets Eat;
So Lovers who profess they Spirits taste,   15
   Feed yet on grosser meat;

I know they boast they Soules to Soules Convey,
How e'r they meet, the Body is the Way.
Come, I will undeceive thee, they that tread
    Those vain Aeriall waies,   20
Are like young Heyrs, and Alchymists misled
    To waste their wealth and Daies,
For searching thus to be for ever Rich,
They only find a Med'cine for the Itch.

ABSENCE

    Fly, O fly sad Sigh, and bear
    These few Words into his Ear;
    'Blest where e'r thou dost remain,
    Worthier of a softer chain,
    Still I live, if it be true   5
    The Turtle lives that's cleft in two:
    Tears and Sorrows I have store,
    But O thine do grieve me more;
    Dye I would, but that I do
    Fear my Fate would kill thee too!   10

CONSIDERATION

Fool that I was, that little of my Span
Which I have sinn'd untill it stiles me Man,
I counted life till now, henceforth I'l say
'Twas but a drowzy lingring, or delay:
Let it forgotten perish, let none tell   5
That I then was, to live is to live well.
Off then thou Old Man, and give place unto
The Ancient of Daies; Let him renew
Mine Age like to the Eagles, and endow
My breast with Innocence, That he whom Thou   10

Hast made a man of sin, and subt'ly sworn
A Vassall to thy Tyranny, may turn
Infant again, and having all of Child,
Want wit hereafter to be so beguild;
O thou that art the way, direct me still   15
In this long tedious Pilgrimage, and till
Thy Voice be born, Lock up my looser Tongue,
He only is best grown that's thus turn'd young.

UPON THE TRANSLATION OF CHAUCER'S TROILUS AND CRESEIDE (INTO LATIN), BY SIR FRANCIS KINASTON

Pardon me Sir, this injury to your Bayes,
That I, who only should admire, dare Praise.
In this great Acclamation to your Name,
I adde unto the noise, though not the Fame.
Tis to your Happy cares wee owe, that wee   5
Read Chaucer now without a Dictionary;
Whose faithfull Quill such constant light affords,
That we now read his thoughts, who read his words,
And, though we know't done in our age by you,
May doubt which is the Coppy of the two.   10
Rome in her Language here beginnes to know
Laws yet untry'd, proud to be fetter'd so;
And, taught our Numbers now at last, is thus
Growne Brittaine yet, and owes one change[1] to us.
The good is common. Hee, that hitherto   15
Was dumbe to strangers, and's owne Country too,
Speakes plainely now to all; being more our owne
Ev'n hence, in that thus made to Aliens knowne.

[1] *charge*, Ed. 1651, Ch.

A TRANSLATION OF HUGO GROTIUS
ELEGY ON ARMINIUS

Arminius Searcher of Truths deepest part,
High Soaring Mind, Pattern of quick-ey'd Art;
Soul big with Learning, Taken from this Blind
And Dusky Age, where Ignorant Mankind
Doth tremble hoodwink'd with uncertain Night;   5
Thou now enjoy'st clear Fields of blessed Light,
And whether that the Truth ows much to thee,
Or as by Nature's Lot Man cannot see
All things, in some part thou didst slip (judge they
Who have that Knowing Pow'r, that holy key)   10
Surely a frequent Reader of that high
Mysterious book, engaged by no tye
To Man's decrees, Heav'n knows thou gain'st from thence
A wary and a Quiet Conscience.
Full both of Rest and Joy in that blest Seat   15
Thou find'st what here thou Sought'st, and seest how great
A Cloud doth muffle Mortals, what a small,
A vain and empty nothing is that All
We here call Knowledge, puff'd with which we Men
Stalk high, oppress, and are oppress'd agen.   20
Hence do these greater wars of Mars arise,
Hence lower Hatreds, mean while Truth far flies,
And that good friend of Holy Peace disdains
To shew her self where strife and tumult raigns:
Whence is this Fury, whence this eager Lust   25
And itch of fighting setled in us? must
Our God become the Subject of our War?
Why sides, so new, so many? hath the Tare
Of the mischievous Enemy by Night

Been scatter'd in Christs fields? or doth the Spight 30
Of our depraved Nature, prone to rage,
Suck in all kind of Fuell, and engage
Man as a Party in Gods Cause? or ought
The Curious World whiles that it suffers nought
To lye obscure, and ransakes every Room 35
Block'd up from Knowledge justly feel this doom?
As that proud Number when they thought to raise
Insolent Buildings, and to reach new waies,
Spread into thousand Languages, and flung
Off the old Concord of their Single Tongue. 40
Alas what's our Intent poor little Flock
Cull'd out of all the world? we bear the Stock
Of new distractions dayly, daily new,
Scoft by the Turk, not pittied by the Jew;
Happy sincere Religion, set apart. 45
As far from Common Faction, as from Art;
Which being sure all Staines are wash'd away
By Christ's large Passion, boldly here doth lay
All Hope and Faith believing that Just One
Bestoweth life, but payes Confusion; 50
Whose practise being Love, cares not to pry
Into the secrets of a Mystery;
Not by an over-anxious Search to know
If future things do come to pass or no,
By a defined Law; how God wills too, 55
Void of't himself, how not, how far our will
Is sweyed by its Mover, what strict Laws
Exercis'd on it by the highest Cause:
And happy he, who free from all by-ends,
Gapes not for filthy Lucre, nor intends 60
The noise of Empty Armour, but rais'd high

To better Cares, minds Heaven; and doth try
To see and know the Deity only there
Where he himself discloseth; and with fear
Takes wary steps in narrow waies, led by   65
The Clew of that good Book that cannot ly:
Who in the midst of Jars walks equall by
An even freedom mix't with Charity:
Whose pure refined Moderation
Condemn'd of all, it self condemneth none;   70
Who keeping Modest Limits now doth please
To speak for truth, now holds his Tongue for Peace;
These things in Publike, these in private too,
These neer thine end, thou Counsail'dst still to do,
Arminius when ev'n suffering decay   75
Under long Cares, weary of further stay
In an unthankful froward Age, when found
Broke in that slighter part, i'th' better sound;
Thou wert enflam'd, and wholly bent to see
Those Kingdoms unto Thousands shewn by thee;   80
And thou a Star now added to the Seat
Of that thy Fathers Temple, dost entreat
God that he give us as much Light as is fit
Unto his Flock, and grant Content with it;
That he give Teachers, such as do not vent   85
Their private Fancies; give a full Consent
Of Hearts, if not of Tongues, and do away
By powerfull fire all dim and base Alay
Of mixt dissensions, that Christ's City be
Link'd and united in one amity;   90
Breath all alike, and being free from strife,
To Heav'n make good their faith, to Earth their life.

LOVE BUT ONE

See these two little Brooks that slowly creep
    In Snaky windings through the Plains,
I knew them once one River, swift and deep,
    Blessing and blest by Poets strains.

Then touch'd with Aw, we thought some God did powr 5
    Those flouds from out his sacred Jar,
Transforming every weed unto a Flow'r
    And every Flower into a Star.

But since it broke it self, and double glides,
    The Naked Banks no dress have worn,   10
And yon dry barren Mountain now derides
    These Valleys which lost glories mourn.

O Chloris! think how this presents thy Love,
    Which when it ran but in one Streame,
We hapy Shepheards thence did thrive and prove, 15
    And thou wast mine and all Mens Theme.

But since't hath been imparted to one more,
    And in two Streams doth weakly creep,
Our Common Muse is thence grown low, and poor,
    And mine as Lean as these my Sheep.   20

But think withall what honour thou hast lost,
    Which we did to thy full Stream pay,
Whiles now that Swain that swears he loves thee most,
    Slakes but his thirst, and goes away?

O in what narrow waies our Minds must move!   25
We may not Hate, nor yet diffuse our Love!

MARTIAL Lib. i. Epic. 66

Ad furem de libro suo

Th'art out, vile Plagiary, that dost think
A poet may be made at th'rate of Ink,
And cheap-priz'd Paper; none e'r purchas'd yet
Six or ten Penniworth of Fame or Wit:
Get Verse unpublish'd, new stamp'd Fancies Look,   5
Which th'only Father of the Virgin Book
Knows, and Keeps seal'd in his close Desk within,
Not slubber'd yet by any ruffer Chin;
A Book, once Known, ne'r quits the Author; if
Any lies yet impolish'd any stiff,   10
Wanting it's Bosses, and it's Cover, do
Get that; I've such, and can be secret too.
    He that repeats stoln Verse, and for Fame looks,
    Must purchase Silence too as well as Books.

MARTIAL Lib. 7. Epig. 60

Ad Jovem capitolinum

Thou Swayer of the Capitoll, whom we
Whiles Caesar's safe, believe a Deity,
Whiles thee with wishes for themselves all tire,
And to be given, what Gods can give, require,
Think me not proud O Jove, 'cause 'mongst the rest 5
I only for myself make no request:
To thee I ought for Caesar's wants alone
To make my Sute, to Caesar for my own.

IN POMPEIOS JUVENES Lib. 5. Epig. 74

Europe and Asia doth th'young Pompeys hold,
He lyes, if any where, in Lybian Mould:
No wonder if in all the world they dwell;
So great a Ruine ne'r in one place fell.

SI MEMINI FUERANT[1] Lib. 1. Epig. 19

To Aelia

Thou hadst four teeth, good Elia, heretofore
But one Cough spit out two, and one two more:
Now thou mayst Cough all day, and safely too;
There's nothing left for the third Cough to do.

MARTIAL Lib. 10. Epig. 5

In maledicum poetam

Who e'r vile slighter of the State, in more
Vile verse, hath libell'd those he should adore,
May be quite banish'd from the Bridge and Hill
Walk through the Streets, and 'mongst hoarse Beggars still
Reserved to the last even then entreat   5
Those mouldy harder Crusts that Dogs won't eat.
A long and wet December, may, what's more,
Stewes shut against him, Keep him cold and poor.
May he proclame those blest, and wish he were
One of the Happy Ones, upon the Bier;   10
And when his slowe houre Comes, whiles yet alive,
May he perceive Dogs for his Carcass strive;
And moving's rags fright eager Birds away:

1 *Si Memine Fuerunt*, Ed. 1651.

Nor let his single torments in death stay;
But deep Gash'd now by Aeacus whips, anon   15
Tasked with the restless Sisyphus his stone,
Then 'mongst the old blabbers waters standing dry;
Weary all Fables, tire all Poetry,
And when a Fury bids him on truth hit,
Conscience betraying him, cry out I writ.   20

MARTIAL Lib. ii. Epic. 18

In Lupum

You gave m'a Mannour, Lupus, but I till
A larger Mannour in my Window still.
A Mannour Call you this? where I can prove
One Sprig of Rew doth make Diana's Grove?
Which a Grasshopper's wing hides? and a small   5
Emmet in one day only eats down all?
An half-blown Rose-leaf Circles it quite round,
In which our Common Grass is no more found,
Than Cosmus Leaf? or unripe Pepper? where
At the full length cann't lye a Cucumber,   10
Nor a whole Snake inhabit? I'm afraid
'Tis with one worm, one Earewick over laid;
The Sallow spent the Gnat yet dies, the whole
Plot without Charge is tilled by the Mole,
A Mushroome cannot open, nor Fig grow,   15
A Violet doth find no room to blow,
A Mouse laies waste the Bounds, my Bayliff more
Doth fear him than the Caledonian Boar[1];
The Swallow in one Claw takes as she flies
The Crop entire, and in her Nest it lies,   20

[1] *Bore*, Ed. 1651, Ch.

No place for half Priapus, though he do
Stand without Syth, and t'other weapon too;
The Harvest in a Cockleshell is put,
And the whole Vintage tunn'd[1] up in a Nut,
Truly but in one Letter, Lupus, thou   25
Mistaken wert; for when thou didst bestow
This Mead confirm'd unto me by thy Seal
I'd rather far th'hadst given me a Meal.

HORAT. CARM. Lib. 4. Ode 13

Audivere Lyce

My Prayers are heard, O Lyce, now
They're heard; years write thee Ag'd, yet thou
    Youthfull and green in will,
    Putt'st in for handsome still,
And shameless dost intrude among   5
The Sports and feastings of the young.

There, thaw'd with Wine, thy ragged throat
To Cupid shakes some feeble Note,
    To move unwilling fires,
    And rouze our lodg'd desires,   10
When he still wakes in Chia's face,
Chia, that's fresh, and sings with Grace.

For he (choice God) doth, in his flight
Skip Sapless Oaks, and will not light
    Upon thy Cheek, or Brow,   15
    Because deep wrinkles now,
Gray Hairs, and Teeth decayed and worn,
Present thee fowl, and fit for scorn.

[1] *turn'd*, Ch.

Neither thy Coan Purples lay,
Nor that thy Jewels native day   20
    Can make thee backwards live,
    And those lost years retrive
Which Winged Time unto our known
And Publike Annals once hath thrown.

Whither is now that Softness flown?   25
Whither that Blush, that Motion gone?
    Alas what now in thee
    Is left of all that She,
That She that loves did breath and deal?
That Horace from himself did steal?   30

Thou wert a while the cry'd-up Face,
Of taking Arts, and catching Grace,
    My Cynara being dead;
    But my fair Cynara's thread
Fates broke, intending thine to draw   35
'Till thou contest with th'Aged Daw.

That those young Lovers, once thy Prey,
'Thy zealous eager Servants, may
    Make thee their Common sport,
    And to thy house resort   40
To see a Torch that proudly burn'd
Now into Colder Ashes turn'd.

ON THE BIRTH OF THE KING'S FOURTH CHILD,
1635

To the Queene

Now that your Princely Birth, Great Queen's so shown
That both Yeares may well clayme it as their owne,
That by this Early Budding we must hate

Times past, and thinke the Spring fell out too late,
Corrected now by You: we aemulous too 5
Bring forth, and with more pangs perhaps than You.
Our Birth takes life, and speech at once, whom we
Have charged here to want no Dictionary.
The former tongue's as hearty and as true;
But that's Your Courts, this onely meant to you. 10

THE SAME: BEING THE PREFACE BEFORE THE ENGLISH VERSES SENT THEM FROM OXFORD

Blest Lady, You, whose Mantle doth divide
The flouds of time swelling on either side,
Your Birth so clos'd the past, yet came so true
A Ciment to that yeare that did ensue,
That Janus did suspect Lucina, least 5
Shee might entrench, and His become Her feast;
Whiles You may challenge one Day, and we doe
Make Time have now two Daughters, Truth and You.
  You bring forth now, great Queen, as you fore-saw
An Antiquation of the Salique Law: 10
T' have shewne once more a Child, whose ev'ry part
May gaine unto our Realme a severall Heart,
So giv'n unto Your King, so fitly sent,
As we may justly call't your Complement.
O for an Angell here to sing! We doe 15
Want such a voice, nay such a Ditty too:
This Cradle too's an Altar, whiles that one
Birth-time combines the Manger and the Throne:
The very Nurse turns Priestesse, and we feare
Will better sing than some grave Poets here. 20

For, now that Royall Births doe come so fast,
That we may feare They'll Commons be at last,
And yet no Plague to cease, no starre to rise,
But those two Twinne-fires onely of Her eyes;
Wits will no more compose, but first Rehearse,   25
And turne the Pray'r of thanks into a Verse;
Some, their owne Plagiaries, will be read
In the Elder statue with a younger Head;
Or, to beare up perhaps an yeelding fame
New-torture old words into Chronogramme;   30
And there may be much concurse to this quill,
For silenc'd Preachers have most Hearers still.
But what dares now to be barren, when our Queene
Transcrib'd is in Her second Copy seene?
Nor is the Father left out there: we may   35
Say those small glasses snatch him ev'ry way:
Which too[1] doe mutually represent
Themselves, as Element doth Element;
Whiles, here, there, yonder, All in All are showne
Casting each others Beauties, and their owne.   40
Your Sonnes, Great Sir, may fix your Scepter here,
But 'tis this sexe must make you raigne elsewhere.
And, though they All be shafts, t'will yet be found
These, though the weaker, make the deeper wound.
Come shee Munition then, and thus appease   45
All clayme, and be the Venus of your Seas:
And henceforth looke we not t'espy from farre
A Guiding light. This be your Navies starre.
And now perhaps You'll thinke a booke more fit,
That, like your Infant's soull, shewes nothing writ.   50
Yet deeme not all our heart spread in this Noise;

[1] *to,* Ch.

The booke would swell, should we but print blanke Joyes:
For we have some that only can rehearse
In Prose, whom Age, and Christmas weanes from verse:
All cannot enter these Poetique lists;   55
This Swath's above the Fillets of some Priests:
And You're so wholly happy, that our Wreath
Must proclaime Blessings only, not Bequeath.

TO MRS DUPPA, SENT WITH THE PICTURE OF THE BISHOP OF CHICHESTER (HER HUSBAND)

IN A SMALL PIECE OF GLASS

A shape for Temple windows fit,
Y'have here in half a quarrell writ,
As Temples are themselves in Spots,
And fairer Cities throng'd in Blots.
Though't fill the World as it doth run,   5
One drop of Light presents the Sun;
And Angels, that whole Nations guide,
Have but a point where they reside.
Such Wrongs redeem themselves, Thus we Confess,
That all expressions of him must be less.   10

Though in those Spots the bounded Sense
Cannot deny Magnificence,
Yet reaching Minds in them may guess
Statues, and Altars, Pyles and Press;
And Fancy seeing more than Sight,   15
May powre that drop to flouds of Light,
And make that point of th' Compass foot
Round, Round into a Center shoot;
The piece may hit to you then, though't be small,
True Love doth find resemblances in all.   20

By Conquer'd Pencils 'tis confess'd
His Actions only draw him best,
Actions that, like these Colours, from
The trying fire more beamy come.
Yet may He still like this appear   25
At one Just stand: Let not the year
Imprint his Brow as it doth run,
Nor known when out, nor when begun;
How ere the shade be, may the Substance long
Confirm't, if right, Confute it, if't be wrong.   30

I was about to say
Ill Omens be away,
All Beasts that Age and Art unlucky stile
Keep from his sight a while;
Let no sad Bird from hollow trees dare preach,   35
Nor men that know less, teach;
And to my self; do you not write
The whole year breaks in this daies Light;
But I am bid blame Fancy, free the thing,
To solid Minds these Trifles no fears bring.   40

I was about to pray
The years good in this day;
That fewer Laws were made, and more were kept,
The Church by Church men swept;
No reall Innovations brought about,   45
To root the seeming out;
And Justice giv'n, nor forc'd by those
Who know not what they do oppose,
But I am taught firme Minds have firmly stood,
And good-wils work for good unto the Good.   50

I was about to Chide
The Peoples raging Tide,
And bid them cease to cry the Bishops down
    When ought did thwart the Town,
Wish'em think Prelates Men, till we did know   55
    How it with Saints would go;
    But I conceiv'd that pious Minds
    Drew deepest sleeps in Storms and Winds;
And could from Tempests gain as quiet Dreams
As Shepheards from the Murmur of small Streams. 60

    And you my Lord, are he,
    Who can all wishes free,
Whose round and solid Mind Knows to Create
    And fashion your own Fate;
Whose firmness can from Ills assure success   65
    Where Others do but guess;
    Whose Conscience holy Calms enjoys
    'Midst the loud Tumults of State-Noise;
Thus gather'd in your self, you stand your own,
Nor rais'd by giddy changes, nor cast down.   70

    And though your Church do boast
    Such (once thought pious) Cost,
That for each Month it shews a severall door,
    You yet do open't More;
Though windows equal weeks, you give't a day   75
    More Bright, more clear than they;
    And though the Pillars which stand there
    Sum up the many hours of th' Year,
The Strength yet, and the Beauty of that frame
Lies not in them so much as in your Name.   80

A Name that shall in Story
Out-shine even Jewels glory
A Name allow'd by all as soon as heard,
  At once both Lov'd and Fear'd,
A Name above all Praise, that will stand high   85
  When Fame itself shall dye,
    Whiles thus your Mind, Pen, Shape, and fit,
    Times to your Vertues will submit,
And Manners unto Times, May Heaven bless thus
All Seasons unto you, and you to us.   90

TO THE KING, ON THE BIRTH OF THE
PRINCESS ANNE[1], MARCH 17th, 1636

Great Sir,

        Successe t'your Royall selfe, and us.
Wee're happy too, in that you're happy thus
For where a Linkt Dependance doth States[2] blesse,
The greaters[3] fortune doth still name the lesse.
Can we be Losers thought, when, for a Ray   5
Or two subtracted, wee've received a Day?
When heav'n, for those few pieces of our Ore
It tooke, sends in th'Elixar to our Store.
And (Mighty Sir) one graine of yours cast in
Turnes all our drossy copper, and our tinne,   10
Hatching to Gold those Mettalls, which the Sunne
It selfe despair'd, and only left begunne.
'Tis then disloyall envy to repine.
W'have lost some Bullion, but have gain'd a Mine.

---

[1] *Elizabeth*, Ed. 1651, but vide note.   [2] *Sates*, Flos Brit. 1636.
[3] *greater*, Ed. 1651, Ch.

If Scepters may have eyes, (as't is not much   15
Amisse to grant them eyes, whose foresight's such)
This Birth so Soveraigne, scatt'ring health each where,
May well be styl'd your Scepter's balsam teare.
Witness that griefe your Queene did late endure,
Blest be that pitty, which doth weep, and cure!   20
Your Issue shewes you now, as in due space
Five glasses justly distant would your face;
Where one still flowing beame illustrates all,
Though by degrees the light doth weaker fall:
And we thus seeing them shall thinke w'have spi'd   25
Your Highnesse only[1] five times multipli'd.
And this proportion'd order makes each one
Only a severall step unto your throne.
Linke thus receiving Linke, may not we men
Say that the Golden Chain's let downe agen,   30
Which by a still succeeding growth doth guide
Unto that Chaire, where the Chain's head is ty'd?
Th'are then Your Selfe lesse copy'd. For as some
By passe, as 'twere, doe send each Vertue home
Unto the Cause, and call it that: so wee   35
Reducing Brookes to Seas, Fruit to the Tree,
Conclude that these are You, Who, when they grow
Up to a ripenesse, will[2] such vertues shew,
That they'll be our example, our rule too;
For they hereafter must doe still as You.   40
Be They then so receiv'd: 'Tis others lot
To have Lawes made; Yours (Greate Sr.) are begot.

[1] *Majesty but*, Ed. 1651, Ch.   [2] *with*, Ch.

TO THE QUEEN:

And something too (great Queene) I was about
For You: but as it stuck, and would not out
(For wee, who have not wit propitious, doe
Travell with verse, and feele our Braine-pangs too)
A nest of Cupid's hov'ring in one bright   5
Cloud, did surprize my fancy, and my sight:
This flock hedg'd in her cradle, and Shee lay
More gracious, more divine, more fresh then they.
Each view'd her eyes, and in her eyes were showne
Darts farre more pow'rfull, though lesse than their owne. 10

    These Venus eyes (says one) these are
Our mothers sparkes, but chaster farre:
And Thetis silver feete are these
The father sure is Lord o' th'seas.
Faire one (saith this) we bring you flow'rs;   15
The Garden one day shall be Yours:
Wear on[1] your Cheekes these; and when you doe
Venture at words, you'll speake'em too.
That veyle that hides great Cupid's eyes
(Saith that) must swath Her as shee lyes.   20
For certaine 't is, that this is shee,
Who destin'd is to make Love see.
Let's pull our wings, that we may drowne
Her gracefull wings in heav'nly downe;
But they so soft are, that I feare   25
Feathers will make impressions there.
May shee with love, and awe be seene,
Whiles ev'ry part presents a Queene;
And thinke, when first shee sees her face,
Her Mother's got behind the glasse.   30

    [1] *We are*, Flos Brit. altered in Ed. 1651, Ch.

This said, a stately maid appear'd, whose sight[1]
Did put the little Archers all to flight:
Her shape was more then humane: such I use
To fancy the most faire, the most chast Muse.
And now by one swift motion being neare   35
My side, shee gently thus did pull mine eare;
Th'emerit ancient warbling Priests, and you
Nothing beyond Collect, or Ballad doe:
Dare you[2] salute a starre without try'd fire?
Or welcome Harmony with an harsher Quire?   40
Raptures are due. Great Goddesse, I leave then,
This subject only doth befit your penne.

UPON THE DRAMATICK POEMS OF
MR JOHN FLETCHER

Though when all Fletcher writ, and the entire
Man was indulged unto that sacred fire,
His thoughts, and his thoughts dresse appeared both such,
That 'twas his happy fault to do too much;
Who therefore wisely did submit each birth   5
To knowing Beaumont e're it did come forth,
Working againe, untille he said 'twas fit,
And made him the sobriety of his wit;
Though thus he call'd his Judge into his fame,
And for that aid allow'd him half the name,   10
'Tis knowne, that sometimes he did stand alone,
That both the Spunge and Pencill were his owne;
That himselfe judged himself, could singly do,
And was at last Beaumont and Fletcher too;

[1] *Light*, Ed. 1651. Ch.   [2] *your*, Ed. 1651.

Else we had lost his Shepheardess, a piece　　　15
Even and smooth, spun from a finer fleece,
Where softnesse raigns, where passions passions greet,
Gentle and high, as flouds of Balsam meet.
Where dress'd in white expressions, sit bright Loves,
Drawne, like their fairest Queen, by milkie Doves;　　20
A piece, which Johnson in a rapture bid.
Come up a glorifi'd work and so it did
　　Else had his Muse set with his friend; the Stage
Had miss'd those Poems. which yet take the Age;
The world had lost those rich exemplars, where　　25
Art, Language, Wit, sit ruling in one Sphere,
Where the fresh matters soar above old Theames,
As Prophets Raptures do above our Dreams;
Where in a worthy scorne he dares refuse
All other Gods, and makes the thing his Muse;　　30
When he calls Passions up[1], and layes them so,
As Spirits aw'd by him to come and go;
When the free Author did what e'r he would,
And nothing will'd, but what a Poet should.
　　No vast uncivill bulk swells any Scene,　　35
The strength's ingenious[2], and the vigour clean;
None can prevent the Fancy, and see through
At the first opening; all stand wond'ring how
The thing will be untill it is, which thence
With fresh delights still cheats, still takes the sence;　40
The whole designe, the shadowes, the lights such
That none can say he shewes or hides too much:
Businesse growes up, ripened by just encrease,
And by as just degrees againe doth cease.

---

[1] *forth*, Ed. 1651, Ch.
[2] *ingenuous*, Ed. 1651, Ch.

The heats and minutes of affairs are watcht,   45
And the nice points of Time are met, and snatcht;
Nought later then it should, nought comes before,
Chymists, and Calculators do erre more;
Sex, age, degree, affections, country, place,
The inward substance, and the outward face,   50
All kept precisely, all exactly fit,
What he would write, he was before he writ.
'Twixt Johnson's[1] grave, and Shakespeare's lighter sound,
His Muse so steer'd that something still was found,
Nor this, nor that, nor both, but so his owne,   55
That 'twas his marke, and he was by it knowne.
Hence did he take true judgements, hence did strike
All Palates some way, though not all alike:
The God of numbers might his numbers crowne,
And listning to them wish they were his owne.   60
    Thus welcome forth, what ease, or wine, or wit,
    Durst yet produce, that is, what Fletcher writ.

ANOTHER ON THE SAME

Fletcher, though some call it thy fault, that wit
So overflow'd thy Scenes, that ere 'twas fit
To come upon the stage, Beaumont was faine
To bid thee be more dull, that's write againe,
And bate some of thy fire, which from thee came   5
In a cleare, bright, full, but too large a flame;
And after all (finding thy Genius such)
That blunted, and allayed, 'Twas yet too much;
Added his sober spunge, and did contract
Thy plenty to lesse wit to make't exact: 10

                    [1] See p. 106, Jonson.

Yet we through his corrections could see
Much treasure in thy superfluity,
Which was so fil'd away, as when we doe
Cut Jewels, that that's lost is jewell too;
Or as men use to wash Gold, which we know   15
By losing makes the stream thence wealthy grow.
They who do on thy workes severely sit,
And call thy store the over-births of wit,
Say thy miscarriages were rare, and when
Thou wert superfluous, that thy fruitfull Pen   20
Had no fault but abundance, which did lay
Out in one Scene what might well serve a Play;
And hence doe grant, that what they call excesse
Was to be reckon'd as thy happinesse,
From whom wit issued in a full spring tide;   25
Much did inrich the Stage, much flow'd beside.
For that thou couldst thine own free fancy binde
In stricter numbers, and run so confin'd
As to observe the rules of Art, which sway
In the contrivance of a true-borne Play,   30
These works proclame, which thou didst write retired
From Beaumont, by none but thy self inspired;
Where we see 'twas not chance that made them hit,
Nor were thy Playes the Lotteries of wit,
But like to Durer's Pencill, which first Knew   35
The laws of faces, and then faces drew:
Thou knowest the air, the colour, and the place,
The simetry, which gives a¹ Poem grace:
Parts are so fitted unto parts, as doe
Shew thou hadst wit, and Mathematicks too;   40
Knewst where by line to spare, where to dispence,

¹ *the*, Ed. 1651, Ch.

And didst beget just Comedies from thence;
Things unto which thou didst such life bequeath,
That they (their own Black Friers) unacted breath.
Johnson hath writ things lasting, and divine,   45
Yet his Love-Scenes, Fletcher, compar'd to thine,
Are cold and frosty, and exprest love so,
As heat with Ice, or warme fires mix'd with Snow;
Thou, as if struck with the same generous Darts,
Which burne, and raigne in noble Lovers hearts,   50
Hast cloath'd Affections in such native tires,
And so describ'd them in their own true fires,
Such moving sighes, such undissembled teares,
Such charms of language, such hopes mixt with feares,
Such grants after denialls, such pursuits   55
After despaire, such amorous recruits,
That some who sat spectators have confest
Themselves transform'd to what they saw exprest,
And felt such shafts through their captived[1] sence
As made them rise Parts, and go Lovers thence.   60
Nor was thy stile wholly composed of Groves,
Or the soft strains of Shepheards and their Loves;
When thou wouldst Comick be, each smiling birth
In that kinde, came into the world all mirth.
All point, all edge, all sharpness; we did sit   65
Sometimes five Acts out in pure sprightfull wit,
Which flow'd in such true salt, that we did doubt
In which Scene we laught most two shillings out.
Shakespeare to thee was dull, whose best jest lyes
I'th' Ladies questions, and the Fooles replyes.   70
Old fashion'd wit, which walk'd from town to town
In turn'd Hose, which our Fathers call'd the Clown;

[1] All editions print *captiv'd*.

Whose wit our nice times would obsceanesse call,
And which made Bawdry pass for Comicall:
Nature was all his Art, thy veine was free   75
As his, but without his scurility;
From whom mirth came unforc'd, no Jest perplext,
But without labour cleane, chaste and unvext.
Thou wert not like some, our small Poets, who
Could not be Poets, were not we Poets too;   80
Whose wit is pilfring, and whose veine and wealth
In Poetry lies meerely in their stealth;
Nor didst thou feel their drought, their pangs, their qualmes,
Their rack in writing, who doe write for almes,
Whose wretched genius, and dependent fires,   85
But to their Benefactors dole aspires.
Nor hadst thou the sly trick, thy selfe to praise
Under thy friends names, or to purchase Bayes
Didst write stale commendations to thy Booke,
Which we for Beaumont's or Ben Johnson's tooke;   90
That debt thou left'st to us, which none but he
Can truly pay[1], Fletcher, who writes like thee.

TO THE RIGHT REVEREND FATHER IN GOD, BRIAN, LORD BISHOP OF CHICHESTER, TUTOR TO THE PRINCE HIS HIGHNESS, MY MOST GRACIOUS PATRON,

Many, and happy daies.

SYRINGUS,   ERGASTUS.

Sy.   Whether so fast Ergastus! say
      Doth Nysa, or Myrtilla stay,
      To meet thee now at Break of Day?

      [1] Most editions have *play*.

Er. With Love, Syringus, I have done,
'Tis duty now that makes me run,   5
To prevent the rising Sun.

Sy. What Star hath chill'd thy flames?
What Cross hath made thy fires take other names?

Er. Didst thou not last night hear
The Dirge we sung to the departed year?   10
'Tis the daies early Prime
That gives new Feet, and Wings to Aged Time,
And I run to provide
Some Rurall present to design the Tide:

Sy. But to whom this Pious fear?   15
To whom this opening of the Year?

Er. To him, that by Thames flowing side
Three Kingdoms Eldest Hopes doth guide,
Who his soft mind and manners Twines,
Gently, as¹ we do tender Vines.   20
'Tis he that sings to him the Course
Of Light, and of the Suns great force,
How his Beams meet, and joyn with Showers,
To awake the sleeping Flowers;
Where Hail, and Snow have each their Treasures; 25
How wandring Stars tread equall Measures,
Ordered as ours upon the Plain,
And how sad Clouds drop down in Rain;
She tells from whence the Loud Wind blows,
And how the Bow of Wonder shews   30
Colours mixt, as in a Loome,
And where doth hang the Thunder's Womb;
How Nature then Cloaths Fields and Woods,
Heaps the high Hills, and pours out Flouds;

¹ *and,* Ed. 1651.

And from thence doth make him run,   35
To what his Ancesters have done,
Then gives some Lesson, which doth say,
What 'tis to shear, and what to Flea,
And shews at last, in Holy Song,
What to the Temple doth belong;   40
What offering suits with every Feast,
And how the Altar's to be drest.

Sy. Now Violets prop his Head,
And soft Flowers make his Bed,
These Blessings he for us prepares,   45
The Joyes of Harvest Crown his Cares.

Er. He labours that we may
Not cast our Pipes away;
That Swords to Plowsheares may be turn'd,
And neither folds, nor Sheep-coats burn'd;   50
That no rude Barbarous Hands
May reap our well grown Lands,
And that, sweet Liberty being barr'd,
We not our Selves become the Heard;
Heaven bless him, and his Books,   55
'Tis he must gild our Hooks,
And for his Charg's Birth-sake, May
Shall be to me one Holy Day.

Sy. Come, I'l along with thee, and joyn,
Some hasty Gift to thine;   60
But we do Pearls, and Amber want,
And pretious Stones are scant.
And how then shall we enter, where
Wealth ushers in the year?

Er. The Berries of the Misseltoe,   65
To him will Orient shew;

And the Bee's Bag as Amber come
From the deep Ocean's Womb;
And Stones which murmuring Waters chide,
Stopt by them as they glide,   70
If giv'n to him, will pretious grow;
Touch him, they must be so.

'Y. I know a Stream, that to the Light
Betraies smooth Pebbles, Black and White;
These I'l present, with which he may   75
Design each Cross and Happy day.

Er. None, none at all of Blacker hue,
Only the White to him are due,
For Heaven, among the Reverend store
Of Learned Men, Loves no one more.   80

3y.   Two days ago
My deep-fleec'd Ewe, should have her Lamb let fall,
   Which if 't be so,
I mean to offer 't to him Dam and all;
   And humbly say   85
I bring a Gift as tender as the Day.

Er.   Name not a Gift,
Who e'r bestows, he still returns him more;
   That's but our Thrift
When he receives, he adds unto our store;   90
   Let's Altars trim,
Wishes are Lambs, and kids, and Flocks to him.

3y.   Let's then the Sun arrest,
And so prolong our duties Feast,
Time will stay till he be blest.   95

Er.   Wish thou to his Charge, and then
I'l wish t'himself, and both agen,
Holy things to holy Men.

Sy. The unvext Earth Flowers to him bring,
And make the year but one great Spring;   100
Let Nature stand, and serve, and wooe,
And make him Prince of Seasons too.

Er.   And his learn'd Guide, no difference know,
And find it one, to Reap and Sow;
Be Harvest all, and he appear   105
As soon i'the Soul, as in the Ear.

Sy.   When his high Charge shall rule the State
(Which Heaven saies shall be, but late)
Let him no Thorns in Manners find,
And in the Many but one Mind;   110
And Plenty pay him so much bliss,
That's Brothers Sheafs bow all to his.

Er. And he that fits him for that Seat,
May he Figs from Thistles eat;
Like Ears of Corn let Men obey,   115
And when he Breaths, bend all one way;
And if that any dare Contest,
Let his Rod still devour the rest.

Sy. Let Rams Change Colour, and behold
Their Fleeces Purple dy'd, or Gold: 120
For this the holy Augur sayes,
Bodes unto kingdoms happy daies.

Er. And his blest Guide like Fortune win,
And die his Flock too, but within;
And, where of Scarlet they be full,   125
Wash he their Souls as white as Wooll.

Sy. Let his Great Scepter discords part,
As once the Staff made Flouds forbear,
And let him by Diviner Art,
Those Tempests into Bulwarks rear;   130

As he who led Men through the deep,
As Shepheards use to Lead their Sheep.

ER. And his Rod sign the easie Flocks,
By being plac'd but in their Sight,
That all their young Ones shew their Locks   135
Ringstreak'd, Speck'd, and mark'd with White;
As that learn'd Man, who Hazell pill'd,
And so by Art his own Flock fill'd.

SY. May his Rich Fleece drink Dew, and Lye
Well drench'd, though all the Earth be Dry.   140

ER. May his Rod bud, and Almonds shew,
Though all the rest do Barren grow.

SY. May he not have a Subject look,
To please with murmuring, as the Brook,
And let the Serpent of the Year   145
Not dare to fix his sharp Teeth here.

ER. May his Guide pull them out, and so
Sow them that they never grow,
Or if in furrows Arm'd they spring,
Death to themselves their weapons bring.   150

Y. May he more Lawrels bring to us,
Than he that set the Calendar thus,
New deeds of glory will appear,
And make his Deeds round as the Year.

ER. And may his Blessed Guide out-live[1]   155
Tears, and himself a new Thread give;
And so his days still fresh transmit,
Doing as time, and Conquering it.

Y. May Vintage joys swell both their Bowrs,

R. And if they o'r flow, O'r flow on Ours.   160

---

[1] *unt-live*, Ed. 1651.

Sy. O would that we, that we, such Prophets were,
As he that slew the Lyon and the Bear.
Er. Credit thyself, our Wishes must prove true,
Far meaner Shepheards have ben Prophets too.

A NEW-YEAR'S GIFT

Although Propriety be Crost,
By those that cry't up most,
No Vote hath yet pass'd to put down
 The pious fires
 Of good desires,   5
Our wishes are as yet our own.

Bless'd be the day then, 'tis New Year's,
 Nature knows no such fears
As those which do our hearts divide,
 In spight of Force   10
 Times keep their Course,
The Seasons run not on their side.

I send my (Muse) to one that knows
 What each Relation ows,
One who keeps waking in his Breast   15
 No other sense
 But Conscience,
That only is his Interest.

Though to be moderate, in this Time,
 Be thought almost a Crime,   20
That vertue yet is his so much,
 That they who make
 All whom they take
Guilty, durst never Call him such.

He wishes Peace, that Publike Good,   25
   Dry Peace, not bought with Blood,
Let such as Honour may maintain,
     And such the Crown
     Would gladly own,
Wish o'er that Wish to him again.   30

He wishes that this Storm subside,
   Hush'd by a turn of Tide,
That one fix'd Calm would smooth the Main,
     As Winds relent
     When Furies spent,   35
O wish that Wish to him again.

The Joys that Solemn Victories Crown,
   When we not slay our own,
Joys that deserve a generall Song
     When the day's gain'd   40
     And no Sword stain'd,
Press on and round him in a Throng.

Thoughts rescue, and his danger kiss'd,
   Being found as soon as miss'd,
With him not taken as before,   45
     Hazard can ne'r
     Make him more dear,
We must not fear so long once more.

Twist then in one most Glorious Wreath
   All Joys you can bequeath,   50
And see them on the Kingdom thrown,
     When there they dwell
     He's pleas'd as well,
As if they sate on him alone.

Go, and return, and for his sake   55
   Less noise and Tumult make,
Than Stars when they do run their Rounds;
    Though Swords and Spears
    Late fill'd his Eares,
He silence Loves, or Gentle Sounds.   60

A NEW-YEAR'S-GIFT TO BRIAN, LORD BISHOP OF SARUM, UPON THE AUTHOR'S ENTRING INTO HOLY ORDERS, 1638

Now that the Village-Reverence doth lye hid,
   As Ægypt's Wisdom did,
In Birds, and Beasts, and that the Tenants Soul,
   Goes with his New-year's fowl:
   So that the Cock, and Hen, speak more   5
   Now, than in Fables heretofore;
    And that the feather'd Things,
    Truly make Love have Wings;
Though we no flying Present have to pay,
A Quill yet snatch'd from thence may sign the Day. 10

But being the Canon bars me Wit and Wine,
   Enjoying the true Vine,
Being the Bayes must yield unto the Cross
   And all be now one Loss,
   So that my Raptures are to steal   15
   And knit themselves in one pure Zeal,
    And that my each day's breath
    Must be a dayly Death;
Without all strain or Fury, I must than
Tell you this New-year brings you a new man.   20

New, not as th'year, to run the same Course o'r
     Which it hath run before,
Lest in the Man himself there be a Round,
     As in his Humor's found,
   And that return seem to make good   25
   Circling of Actions, as of Bloud;
     Motion as in a Mill
     Is busie standing still;
And by such wheeling we but thus prevaile,
To make the Serpent swallow his owne Taile.   30

Nor new by solemnizing looser Toyes
     And erring with less Noyse,
Taking the Flag and Trumpet from the Sin,
     So to offend within.
   As some Men silence loud Perfumes   35
   And draw them into shorter Rooms,
     This will be understood
     More wary, not more Good.
Sins too may be severe, and so no doubt
The Vice but only sowr'd, not rooted out.   40

But new, by th'Using of each part aright,
     Changing both Step and Sight,
That false Direction come not from the Eye,
     Nor the foot tread awry,
   That neither that the way aver,   45
   Which doth tow'rd Fame, or Profit err,
     Nor this tread that Path, which
     Is not the right, but Rich;
That thus the Foot being fixt, thus lead the Eye,
I pitch my Walk low, but my Prospect high.   50

New too, to teach my Opinions not t'submit
    To Favour, or to Wit,
Nor yet to Walk on Edges, where they may
    Run safe in Broader way;
    Nor to search out for New Paths, where   55
    Nor Tracks nor Footsteps doth appear,
      Knowing that Deeps are waies,
      Where no Impression staies,
Nor servile thus, nor curious, may I then
Approve my Faith to Heaven, my Life to Men.   60

But I who thus present my self as New,
    Am thus made New by You,
Had not your[1] Rayes dwelt on me, One long Night
    Had shut me up from Sight;
    Your Beams exhale me from among   65
    Things tumbling in the Common Throng,
      Who thus with your fire burns
      Now gives not, but Returns;
To Others then be this a day of Thrift
They do receive, but you Sir make the Gift.   70

TO THE QUEENE, AFTER HER DANGEROUS DELIVERY, 1638

Great Madam,
    Though we could wish Your Issue so throng'd stood,
That all the Court were but one Royall Blood;
Though Your Young Jewels be of so much Cost,
That Your Least Spark of Light must not be lost:
Yet when t'Your Burthens Heaven not permits   5

---

[1] *you're*, Ed. 1651.

Quiets[1], as husht, as when the Halcyon sits;
And that Y'are thought so stor'd, that You may spare
Some Glories, and allow Blest Saints a share;
Contentedly we suffer such a Crosse,
T'endeare the Tablet by a Copies losse: 10
And (as in urgent Tempests 'tis a Taught
Thrift, to redeeme the Vessell with the[2] Fraught)
We doe halfe-willing with th'Elixir part
To keep the Alembeck safe for future Art:
Our Treasure thus is shared by the Birth,   15
Halfe unto Heaven, Halfe unto[3] the Earth.

   Come[4] Your Escape as Issue then, whiles we
Receive Your Safety as New Progeny:
Be You from henceforth to us a New Vow,
By Vertues Deare Before, by Danger Now.   20
Twice[5] giv'n, and yet no narrownesse of Thrift;
What ere[6] is Great, may be a Second Guift;
Thus when the Best Act's done, there doth remaine
This only, to performe that Act againe.

   See how Your Great just Consort bears the Crosse! 25
Your Safeties Gaine makes him oresee the Losse:
So that although this Cloud stand at the Doore,
His Great Designes goe on still as before.
Thus stout Horatius being ready now
To dedicate a Temple, and by Vow   30
Settle Religion to his God, although
'Twas told his Child was dead, would not let goe
The Post o'th' Temple, but unmov'd Alone
Bid them take care o'th' funerall, and went on.

---

[1] *Quiet,* Ed. 1651, Ch.   [2] *a,* ibid.
[3] *th'other Halfe,* ibid.   [4] *Came,* ibid.
[5] *Well,* ibid.   [6] *What be,* ibid.

ON THE DEATH OF THE RIGHT HONOURABLE VISCOUNT BAYNING

So when[1] an hasty vigour doth disclose
An early flame in the more forward[2] Rose,
That rarenesse doth destroy it; Wonders owe
This to themselves still, that they cannot grow.
Such Ripenesse was His Fate; Thus to appeare   5
At first, was not hereafter to stay here.
Who thither first steps, whither[3] others tend,
When He sets forth is at the journey's end.

But as Short things most vigour have, and we
Find Force the Recompence of Brevity;   10
So was it here: Compactednesse gave Strength,
The Life was Close, though not spun out at Length.
Nothing lay idle in't: Experience Rules,
Men strengthen'd Books, & Cities season'd schools.

Nor did he issue forth to come Home thence   15
(As some) lesse Man, than they goe out from hence:
Who think new Ayre new Vices may create,
And stamp sinne Lawful in Another State;
Who make Exotick Customes Native Arts,
And loose Italian Vices English Parts: 20
He naturaliz'd Perfections only; gain'd
A round and solid mind, severely train'd,
And manag'd his desires; brought oft checkt Sense
Unto the sway of Reason, comming thence
His owne acquaintance, morgag'd unto none,   25
But was himselfe His owne possession.

---

[1] *where*, Ed. 1651, Ch.   [2] *froward*, ibid.
[3] *whether*, Ed. 1651.

Thus starres by journying still, gaine, and dispense,
Drawing at once, and shedding influence:
Thus Spheares by Regular Motion doe increase
Their times, and bring their Discords into Peace.   30
    Hence knew He his owne value, ne're put forth
Honour for Merit; Pow'r instead of Worth:
Nor, when He poyz'd himselfe, would he prevaile
By wealth, and make his Mannors turne the scale.
Desert was only ballanc'd; nor could we   35
Say my Lord's Rents were only weight, not He:
Only one slight he had; from being Small
Unto himselfe, He came Great unto all:
But Great by no mans Ruine: For who will
Say that his Seat e're made the next Seate ill: 40
No Neighb'ring-village was unpeopled here
'Cause it durst bound a Noble Eye too neere.
Who could e're say my Lord, and the next Marsh
Made frequent Herriots? or that any harsh
Oppressive usage made Young Lives soone fall?   45
Or who could His seven thousand bad Ayre call?
He blessings shed; Men knew not to whom more,
The Sun, or Him, they might impute their store.
No rude exaction, or licentious times
Made his Revenewes Others, or His Crimes: 50
Nor are his Legacies poore-mens present teares,
Or doe they for the future raise their feares.
No such contrivance here as to professe
Bounty, and with Large Miseries feed the Lesse;
Fat some with their owne almes; bestow, and pill;   55
And common Hungers with Great Famines[1] fill,
Making an Hundred Wretches endow 'Tenne,

---

[1] *Famine*, Ed. 1651, Ch.

Taking the Field, and giving a Sheafe then:
As Robbers, whom they spoile[1], perhaps will lend
Small summes to helpe them to their journey's end.   60
All was untainted here, and th'Author such,
That every gift from Him grew twice as much.

We, who erewhile did boast his presence, doe
Now boast a second grace, his bounty too;
Bounty, was judgment here: for he bestowes   65
Not who disperseth, but who gives and knowes.
And what more wise designe, then to renew,
And dresse the brest, from which[2] he knowledge drew!
Thus pious men, ere their departure, first
Would crown the fountain which had quencht their thirst. 70
Hence strive we all his memory to engrosse,
Our Common Love before, but now our Losse.

IN MEMORY OF THE MOST WORTHY
BENJAMIN JOHNSON[3]

Father of Poets, though thine own great day
Struck from thy selfe, scornes that a weaker ray
Should twine in lustre with it: yet my flame,
Kindled from thine, flies upwards tow'rds thy Name.
For in the acclamation of the lesse   5
There's Piety, though from it no accesse.
And though my ruder thoughts make me of those,
Who hide and cover what they should disclose;
Yet, where the lustre's such, he makes it seene
Better to some, that drawes the veile betweene.   10

---

[1] *they've spoyl'd*, Ed. 1651, Ch.
[2] *whence*, ibid.
[3] The old spelling of Ben Jonson's name.

And what can more be hop'd, since that divine
Free filling spirit tooke[1] its flight with thine?
Men may have fury, but no raptures now;
Like witches, charme, yet not know whence, nor how,
And through distemper, grown not strong but fierce;   15
In stead of writing, only rave in verse:
Which when by thy Lawes judg'd 'twill be confess'd,
'Twas not to be inspir'd, but be posses'd.
Where shall we find a Muse like thine, that can
So well present and shew man unto man,   20
That each one finds his twin, and thinkes thy Art
Extends not to the gestures, but the heart?
Where one so shewing life to life, that we
Think thou taughtst Custome, and not Custome thee?
Manners, that were Themes[2] to thy Scenes still flow   25
In the same streame, and are their comments now:
These times thus living o're thy Modells, we
Thinke them not so much wit, as prophesie:
And though we know the character, may sweare[3]
A Sybill's finger hath bin busie there.   30
    Things common thou speakst proper, which though
        showne
For publique, stampt by thee grow thence thine owne:
Thy thoughts so order'd, so express'd, that we
Conclude that thou didst not[4] discourse, but see
Language so master'd, that thy numerous feet,   35
Laden with genuine words, doe alwaies meet
Each in his art; nothing unfit doth fall,
Shewing the Poet, like the wise man[5], All:

[1] takes, Ed. 1651, Ch.
[2] Manners were Themes, and, ibid.   [3] may and swear, ibid.
[4] nor, Ed. 1651.   [5] men, Ed. 1651, Ch.

Thine equall skill thus wresting nothing, made
Thy penne seeme not so much to write as trade.   40
   That life, that Venus of all things, which we
Conceive or shew, proportion'd decencie,
Is not found scattred in thee here and there,
But, like the soule, is wholly every where.
No strange perplexed maze doth passe for plot,   45
Thou alwayes doth unty, not cut the knot.
Thy Lab'rinths doores are open'd by one thread
That[1] tyes, and runnes through all that's don or said.
No power comes down with learned hat and[2] rod,
Wit onely, and contrivance is thy god.   50
   'Tis easie to guild gold: there's small skill spent
Where ev'n the first rude masse is ornament:
Thy Muse tooke harder metalls, purg'd and boild,
Labour'd and try'd, heated, and beate and toyld,
Sifted the drosse, fil'd roughnes, then gave dresse,   55
Vexing rude subjects into comelinesse.
Be it thy glory then, that we may say,
Thou run'st where th'foote was hindred by the way.
   Nor dost thou poure out, but dispence thy veine,
Skill'd when to spare, and when to entertain: 60
Not like our wits, who into one piece do
Throw all that they can say, and their friends too.
Pumping themselves, for one Termes noise so dry,
As if they made their wills in Poetry.
And such spruce compositions presse the stage,   65
When men transcribe themselves and not the age.
Both sorts of Playes are thus like pictures showne,
Thine of the common life, theirs of their owne.
Thy modells yet are not so fram'd, as we

[1] *Which*, Ed. 1651, Ch.   [2] *or*, ibid.

May call them libells, and not imag'rie.   70
No name on any Basis: 'tis thy skill
To strike the vice, but spare the person still:
As he, who when he saw the Serpent wreath'd
About his sleeping sonne, and as he breath'd,
Drinke in his soule, did so the shoote contrive,   75
To kill the beast, but keepe the child alive.
So dost thou aime thy darts, which, ev'n when
They kill the poisons, do but wake the men.
Thy thunders thus but purge, and we endure
Thy lanncings better than anothers cure;   80
And justly too; for th'age growes more unsound
From the fooles balsam, then the wise mans wound.
   No rotten talke brokes[1] for a laugh; no page
Commenc'd man by th'instructions of thy stage;
No bargaining line there; no provoc'tive verse;   85
Nothing but what Lucretia might rehearse;
No need to make good count'nance ill, and use
The plea of strict life for a looser Muse;
No Woman rul'd thy quill: we can descry
No verse borne under any Cynthia's eye;   90
Thy Starre was judgement onely, and right sense,
Thy selfe being to thy selfe an influence.
Stout beauty is thy grace; Sterne pleasures do
Present delights, but mingle horrours too:
Thy Muse doth thus like Joves fierce girle appeare,   95
With a faire hand, but grasping of a Speare.
   Where are they now that cry, thy Lampe did drinke
More oyle than th'Author wine, while he did thinke?
We do imbrace their slannder: thou hast writ
Not for dispatch but fame; no market wit;   100

----

[1] *breaks*, Ed. 1651, Ch.

'Twas not thy care, that it might passe and sell,
But that it might endure, and be done well;
Nor would'st thou venture it unto the eare,
Untill the file would not make smooth, but weare;
Thy verse came season'd hence, and would not give;   105
Borne not to feed the Authour, but to live;
Whence 'mong the choycer Judges rise[1] a strife,
To make thee read as[2] Classick in thy life.
Those that doe hence applause, and suffrage begge,
'Cause they can Poems forme upon one legge,   110
Write not to time, but to the Poets day:
There's difference between fame, and sudden pay.
These men sing kingdomes falls, as if that fate
Us'd the same force t'a Village, and a State:
These serve Thyestes bloody supper in,   115
As if it had onely a ballad bin:
Their Catalines are but Fencers, whose fights rise
Not to the fame of battell, but of prize.
But thou still put'st true passion on; dost write
With the same courage that try'd Captaines fight;   120
Giv'st the right blush and colour unto things;
Low without creeping, high without losse of wings;
Smooth, yet not weake, and by a thorough-care,
Bigge without swelling, without painting faire:
They wretches, while they cannot stand to fit,   125
Are not wits, but materialls of wit.
What though thy searching wit[3] did rake the dust
Of time, and purge old mettalls of their rust?
It is no labour, no art, thinke they, to
Snatch Shipwracks from the deepe, as Dyvers do?   130

[1] *rose*, Ed. 1651, Ch.   [2] *a*, ibid.
[3] *Muse*, ibid.

And rescue Jewells from the covetous sand,
Making the Seas hid wealth adorne the Land?
What though thy calling Muse did rob the store
Of Greeke, and Latine gardens to bring o'r[1]
Plants to thy native soyle? Their vertues were   135
Improv'd farre more, by being planted here.
If thy Skill to their essence doth refine
So many drugges, is not the water thine?
Thefts thus become just works: they and their grace
Are wholly thine: thus doth the stampe and face   140
Make that the Kings, that's ravisht from the mine:
In others then 'tis oare, in thee 'tis coine.
   Blest life of Authours, unto whom we owe
Those that we have, and those that we want too:
Th'art all so good, that reading makes thee worse,   145
And to have writ so well's thine only curse.
Secure then of thy merit, thou didst hate
That servile base dependence upon fate;
Successe thou ne'r thoughtst vertue, nor that fit,
Which chance, and[2] th'ages fashion did make hit;   150
Excluding those from life in after-time,
Who into Po'try first brought luck and rime:
Who thought the peoples breath good ayre: styl'd name
What was but noise; and getting Briefes for fame
Gathered the many's suffrages, and thence   155
Made commendation a benevolence;
Thy thoughts were their owne Lawrell, and did win
That best applause of being crown'd within.
   And though th'exacting age, when deeper yeares
Had interwoven snow among thy haires,   160

---

[1] *ore* and full stop, in J.V.
[2] *or*, Ed. 1651, Ch.

Would not permit thou shouldst grow old, cause they
Nere by thy writings knew thee young; we may
Say justly, they're ungratefull, when they more
Condemn'd thee, cause thou wert so good before:
Thine Art was thine Arts blurre, and they'll confesse   165
Thy strong perfumes made them not smell thee lesse,
But, though to erre with thee be no small skill,
And we adore the last draughts of thy Quill;
Though these thy thoughts, which the now queasie age,
Doth count but clods, and refuse of the stage,   170
Will come up Porcelaine-wit some hundreds hence,
When there will be more manners, and more sense;
'Twas judgement yet to yield, and we afford
Thy silence as much fame, as once thy word;
Who like an aged oake, the leaves being gone,   175
Wast food before, and now religion;
Thought still more rich, though not so richly stor'd,
View'd and enjoy'd before, but now ador'd.
    Great soule of numbers, whom we want and boast;
Like curing gold, most valu'd now th'art lost;   180
When we shall feed on refuse offalls, when
We shall from corne to akornes turne agen;
Then shall we see that these two names are one,
Johnson and Poetry, which now are gone.

A NEW-YEAR'S GIFT TO A NOBLE LORD, 1640

My Lord,

    Though the distemper'd Many cry they see
        The Missall in our Liturgie:
    The Almanack that is before it set
        Goes true, and is not Popish yet.

Whiles therefore none indites   5
   This feast of Roman Rites,
Whiles as yet New-Year in Red Paint,
   Is not cry'd out on for a Saint;
Presents will be no Offrings, and I may
Season my duty safely with the day.   10

Now an Impartiall Court, deaf to Pretence,
   Sits like the Kingdoms Conscience,
While Actions now are touch'd, and Men are try'd,
   Whether they can the day abide,
      Though they should go about   15
      To track Offences out,
   In Deeds, in Thoughts, without, within,
   As Casuists, when they search out Sin;
When Others shake, how safe do you appear,
And a just Patriot know no private fear?   20

This you have gain'd from an unbiass'd Breast,
   Discharg'd of all Self-Interest;
From Square, and Solid Actions without flaw,
   That will in time themselves grow Law,
      Actions that shew you mean   25
      Nought to the Common Scene,
   That you'l n'er lengthen power by Lust,
   But shape and size it by your Trust,
That you do make the Church the Main, no Bye,
And chiefly mean what Others but Apply.   30

Were every Light thus Regular as you,
   And to it's destin'd Motions true,
Did some not shine too short, but reach about,
   And throw their wholesome Lustre out,

What danger then or fear,   35
  Would seize this Sacred Sphere?
Who would impute that Thriving Art
  That turns a Charge into a Mart?
We would enjoy, like you, a State Confess'd
Happy by all, still Blessing, and still Bless'd.   40

But whether false suspicion, or true Crimes
  Provoke the Sowreness of the Times;
Whether't be Pride, or Glory call'd Pride, all
  Expect at least some sudden fall;
    And seeing as Vices, so   45
    Their Cures may too far go,
  And Want of Moderation be
  Both in the Ill, and Remedy,
So that perhaps to bar th'Abuse of Wine
Their Zeal may lead them to cut up the Vine.   50

Pray'rs are Our Arms; and the time affords
  On a Good Day be said Good Words;
Could I shape Things to Votes, I'd wish a Calm
  Soveraign, and soft as Flouds of Balm;
    But as it is, I square   55
    The Vote to the Affair,
  And with this Storm may shake the Vine,
  Only to make it faster twine;
That hence the Early Type may be made good,
And our Ark too, rise higher with the Floud.   60

As then Sick Manners call forth wholsome Laws,
  The Good effect of a bad Cause,
So all I wish must settle in this Sum,
  That more strength from Laxations come.

But how can this appear   65
To humor the New Year?
When proper Wishes, fitly meant,
Should breath his Good to whom they're sent.
T'have a large Mind (my Lord) and that assures,
To wish the Publike Good, is to wish Yours.   70

UPON THE BIRTH OF THE KING'S
SIXTH CHILD, 1640

reat Mint of Beauties:
    Though all Your Royall Burthens should come forth
ischarged by Emanation, not by Birth;
hough You could so prove Mother, as the Soule,
/hen it doth most conceive without controule;   5
hough Princes should so frequent from You flow,
hat we might thence say, Sun-Beames issue slow;
ay, though those Royall Plants as oft should spring
rom You, as great Examples from Your King;
one would repine, or, Narrow[1] midst such Store,   10
hinke the Thrones Blessing made the Kingdome Poore.
raynes, which are singly Rich, become not Cheape
ecause th'are Many: Such grow from the Heape.
hen Five would Each for Number passe Alone,
he Sixth comes Their Improvement, and its Owne.   15
'e see the Brothers Vertues, growing ripe
y just degrees, aspire to their Great Type;
'e see the Father thrive in Them, and finde
'have Heires, as to His Throne, so to His Mind:
his makes us call for More: the Parents Bloud   20
 great security, They will be Good.

[1] *murmur*, Ed. 1651, Ch.

And These Your Constant Tributes to the State
Might make us stand up High, and trample Fate;
We might grow Bold from Conscience of just Good,
Had it the fortune to be Understood.   25
But Some, that would see, dazzled by[1] much light,
View only that which doth confound their sight:
Others, darke by Designe, doe veyle their eyes,
For feare by their own fault they should grow Wise,
And, what they cannot misse, by chance should finde: 30
Injustice[2] is, what Justice should be, Blind.
Yet our Great Guide, carelesse of Common Voyce,
As Good by Nature rather, than by Choyce,
Sheds the same fruitfull Influence still on All,
As constant Show'rs on Thanklesse Deserts fall: 35
And, like the Unmov'd Rock, though it doth heare
The Murmurs of Rude Waves, whose Rage breakes there;
He still gives Living Gemms, and doth present
To Froward Nations Wealth, and Ornament.
Some Stones there are, whose Colours doe betray   40
The Face of Heaven, and that Scene of Day
That Nature shap'd them in, and thence come forth
Themselves th'Ingenuous[3] Records of their Birth.
May then this Pearle (Great Queene) now bred from You;
Congeald, and fashioned of more Heavenly Dew,   45
Shew forth the Temper of the Present State,
And Himselfe be to his owne Birth the Date:
That, as the solemne Trumpet's publique Blast
At the same time proclaim'd both Warre and Fast,
He may, Devoutly Valiant, praying stand,   50
As the Ancient Heroes, with a Speare in's hand;

---

[1] *with*, Ed. 1651, Ch.   [2] *In justice*, ibid.
[3] *ingenious*, ibid.

And, mixing Vowes and Fights in one Concent,
Divide Himselfe between the Church, and Tent:
But if He be, by Milder Influence, born
The Sonne of Peace, the Rose without a Thorne;   55
What once His Grand-sire's Ripe Designes did boast;   .
And Now His Serious Father labours most;
Hee, as a Pledge sent to Both Nations, doe;
And cement Kingdoms, now againe call'd Two.
    And here some Genius prompt me, I shall see   60
Him make Greeke Fables Brittish History;
And view, now such a Goddesse hath[1] brought forth,
This Floating Island setled by the Birth.

UPON THE DEATH OF THE MOST HOPEFULL
THE LORD STAFFORD[2]

Must then our Loves be short still? Must we choose
Not to enjoy? Onely admire, and loose?
Must Axioms hence grow sadly understood,
And we thus see, 'Tis "dangerous to be good"?
So Bookes begunne are broken off, and we   5
Receive a fragment for an History;
And, as 'twere present wealth, what was but debt,
Lose that, of which we were[3] not Owners yet;
But as in bookes, that want the closing line,
We onely can conjecture, and repine;   10
So must we heere too onely grieve, and guesse,
And by our fancy make, what's wanting, lesse.
Thus when rich webs are left unfinished,

[1] *that*, Ed. 1651, Ch.
[2] *the last of his name*, P.B.   [3] *are*, ibid.

The Spider doth supply them with her[1] thred,
For tell me what addition can be wrought   15
To him, whose Youth was even the bound of thought;
Whose buddings did deserve the Robe, whiles we
In smoothnesse did the deeds of wrinckles see:
When his state-nonage might have beene thought fit,
To breake the custome, and allow'd to sit?   20
His actions veil'd his age, and could not stay
For that which we call ripenesse, and just day.
Others may waite the staffe, and the gray haire,
And call that Wisedome, which is onely Feare,
Christen a coldnesse, temp'rance, and then boast   25
Full and Ripe Vertue[2] when all action's lost:
[3] Had he then liv'd; Pow'r ne'r had been thought short
That could not Crush, taught only to support.
No Poor-man's Sighs had been the Lord's Perfumes,
No Tenants Nakedness had hung his Rooms,   30
No Tears had sowr'd his wines, no tedious, Long-
Festivall-service been the Countri's wrong;
A Wretch's Famine had been no dish then,
Nor Greatness thought to eat no Beasts, but Men;
Nor had that been esteem'd a Politick Grace   35
When Sutors came to shew a serious Face;
Or when an humble Cosen did pass by,
Put saving Bus'ness in his frugall Eye;
Things of Injustice then and Potent Hate
Had not been done for th'profit of the State;   40
Nor had it been the Privilege of High Bloud
To back their Injuries with the Kingdom's good:

---

[1] *his*, Ed. 1651, Ch.   [2] *Vertues*, ibid.
[3] This passage down to *Instruments and Men* (l. 44) is omitted in
H. and V. and P.B.

Servants and Engines had been two things then,
And difference made 'twixt Instruments and Men.
This is not to be noble, but be slacke: 45
A Stafford ne're was good[1] by the Almanack.
He, who thus stayes the season, and expects,
Doth not gaine habits, but disguise defects.
Heere Nature outstrips[2] Culture: He came try'd;
Strait of himselfe at first, not rectified: 50
Manners so pleasing, and so handsome cast,
That still that overcame, that was shewne[3] last:
All mindes were captiv'd thence, as if 'thad beene
The same to him, to have been lov'd, and seene.
Had he not bin snatched thus, what drive[4] hearts now   55
Into his nets, would have driven Cities too:
For these his Essaies, which began to win,
Were but bright sparks, which shew'd the Mine within,
Rude draughts unto the picture; things we may
Stile the first beames of the increasing day;   60
Which did but onely great discoveries bring,
As outward coolenesse shewes the inward spring.
Nor were his actions, to content the sight,
Like Artists Pieces, plac'd in a good light,
That they might take at distance, and obtrude   65
Something unto the eye that might delude:
His deeds did all most perfect then appeare,
When you observ'd, view'd close, and did stand neere,
For could there ought else spring from him, whose line
From which[5] he sprung, was rule, and discipline.   70
Whose Vertues were as Bookes before him set,

---

[1] *And to be good only*, Ed. 1651, Ch.   [2] *outstrip'd*, ibid.
[3] *which was seen*, ibid.   [4] *drove*, ibid., *drive*, P.B.
[5] *whence*, Ed. 1651, Ch.

So that they did instruct, who did beget,
Taught thence not to be powerfull, but know,
Shewing he was their blood by living so.
For, whereas some are by their bigge lippe knowne,   75
Others b'imprinted burning swords were showne:
So they by great deeds are, from which bright fame,
Engraves free reputation on their name:
These are their Native markes, and it hath bin
The Staffords lot, to have their signes within.   80
And though this firme Hereditary good,
Might boasted be, as flowing with the blood,
Yet he nere graspt this stay: But as those, who
Carry perfumes about them still, scarce doe
Themselves perceive them, though anothers sense   85
Sucke in th'exhaling odours: so he thence
Ne'r did perceive he carry'd this good smell,
But made new still by doing himselfe well.
T'embalme him then is vaine, where spreading fame
Supplies the want of spices; where the Name,   90
It selfe preserving, may for Ointments passe:
And he, still seene, lye coffind as in glasse.
Whiles thus his bud dims full flowres[1], and his sole
Beginning doth reproach anothers whole,
Comming so perfect up, that there must needes   95
Have beene found out new Titles for new deeds;
Though youth, and lawes forbid, which will not let
Statues be rais'd, or him stand Brasen: yet
Our mindes retaine this Royalty of Kings,
"Not to be bound to time," but judge of things,   100
And worship, as they merit: there we doe
Place him at height, and he stands golden too.

[1] *is full Flower*, Ed. 1651, Ch.

A comfort, but not equall to the crosse,
A faire remainder, but not like the losse:
For he, that[1] last pledge, being gone, we doe   105
Not onely lose the Heire but th'Honour too.
Set we up then this boast against our wrong,
He left no other signe, that he was young:
And, spight of fate, his living vertues will,
Though he be dead, keepe up the Barony still.   110

TO MY HONOUR'D FRIEND MR THOMAS KILLI-GREW, ON HIS PLAYES, *THE PRISONERS* AND *CLARACILLA*

Worthy Sir,

Manners, and Men, transcrib'd, Customes express'd,
The Rules, and Lawes Dramatique[2] not transgress'd;
The Points of Place, and Time, observ'd, and hit;
The Words to Things, and Things to Persons fit;
The Persons constant to Themselves throughout;   5
The Machin turning free[3], not forc'd about;
As Wheeles by Wheeles, part mov'd, and urg'd by part;
And choyce Materials workt with choycer Art;
These, though at last begg'd from long sweate & toyle,
Fruits of the Forge, the Anvil, and the File,   10
Snatch reverence from our Judgements; and we doe
Admire those Raptures with new Raptures too.
But you, whose thoughts are Extasies; who know
No other Mold, but that you'll cast it so;
Who in an even web rich fancies twist,   15

---

[1] *the*, Ed. 1651, Ch.

[2] *Dragmatique*, Ed. 1651.   [3] *fire*, Ed. 1651, Ch.

Your selfe th'Apollo, to your selfe, the Priest;
Whose first unvext conceptions do come forth,
Like Flowers with Kings Names, stampt with Native worth;
By Art unpurchas'd make the same things thought
Far greater when begot, than when they're Taught.   20
So the Ingenuous fountaine clearer flowes
And yet no food besides its owne spring knowes.
    Others great gathering wits there are who like
Rude Scholers, steale this posture from Van Dike[1].
That hand, or eye from Titian, and doe than   25
Draw that a blemish was design'd a Man;
(As that which goes in Spoyle and Theft, we see
For th'most part comes out Impropriety)
But here no small stolne parcells slily lurke,
Nor are your Tablets such Mosaique worke,   30
The web, and woofe are both your owne, the peece
One, and no sayling for the Art, or fleece,
All's from your Selfe, unchalleng'd All, All so,
That breathing Spices doe not freer flow.
No Thrifty Spare, or Manage of dispence,   35
But things hurld out with Gracefull Negligence,
A generous Carriage of unwrested wit;
Expressions, like your Manners freely fit:
No Lines, that wracke the Reader with such guesse,
That some interpret Oracles with lesse.   40
Your Writings are all Christall, such as doe
Please Critiques palates without Critiques too:
You have not what diverts some Men from sense,
Those two Mysterious things, Greeke and Pretence:
And happily you want those shadowes, where   45
Their Absence makes your Graces seeme more cleare.

[1] *Dick*, Ed. 1651, Ch.

Nor are you he, whose vow weares out a Quille
In writing to the Stage, and then sits still,
Or as the Elephant breeds (once in ten yeares,
And those ten yeares but once) with labour beares   50
A secular play. But you goe on and show
Your veine is Rich and full, and can still flow;
That this doth open, not exhaust your store,
And you can give yet two, and yet two more,
Those great eruptions of your beames do say,   55
When others Sunnes are set, you'le have a Day.
And if Mens approbation be not Lot,
And my prophetique Bayes seduce me not;
Whiles he, who straines for swelling scenes, lyes dead
Or onely prays'd you shall live prays'd, and read.   60
   Thus, trusting to your selfe, you Raigne; and doe
   Prescribe to others, because none to you.

THE MARRIAGE OF LADY MARY TO THE PRINCE OF AURANGE HIS SON, 1641

Amids such Heate of Businesse, such State-throng
      Disputing Right and Wrong,
And the sowre tustle of Unclosed Affaires;
     What meane those Glorious Payres?
   That Youth? That Virgin? Those All Dresst?   5
   The Whole, and every Face, a Feast?
      Great Omen! O ye Pow'rs,
      May this Your knot be Ours!
Thus while[1] Cold things with Hot did jarre,
And Dry with Moyst made Mutuall Warre,   10
      Love from that Masse did leap;
     And what was but an Heap
    [1] *where* Ed. 1651, Ch.

Rude and Ungatherd, swift as thought, was hurld
Into the Beauty of an Ordred world.

Goe then into His Arms, New as the Morne, 15
        Tender as Blades of Corne,
Soft as the wooll, that Nuptiall Posts did crowne,
       Or th'Hallowd Quinces Downe,
    That Rituall Quince, which Brides did eate,
  When with their Bridegrooms they would treate. 20
        Though You are Young as th'Howres
        Or This fresh Month's first Flowres:
Yet, if Love's Priests can ought discerne,
Fayrest, You are not now to learne,
        What Hopes, what Sighs, what Teares, 25
        What Joyes are, or what Feares
Ere Time to Lower Soules doth Motion bring,
The Great break out, and of Themselves take wing.

And You, Great Sir, 'mongst Speares and Bucklers borne,
        And by Your Father sworne 30
To worke the Webbe of His Designes compleate;
        Yeld to this Milder Heate.
    Upon the same Rich Stock, we know,
    Valour, and Love, Both[1] Planted grow:
        But Love doth first inspire 35
        The Soule with his soft Fire,
Chasing the Brest for Noble Deeds;
Then in That Seat True Valour breeds.
        So Rocks first yield a Teare,
        Then Gemms that will not weare. 40
So, oft, the Groecian's Sword did first divide
His Bridall Cake, then pierce the Enemies Side.

        [1] *doth*, Ed. 1651, Ch.

D'You see? or am I false? Your[1] Tender Vine,
  Me thinks, on every twine
Tiaras, Scepters, Crownes, Spoyles, Trophies weares,   45
  And such Rich Burthens beares,
 Which, hanging in their Beauteous shapes,
 Adorn her Bowghs like swelling Grapes:
  But Time forbids the Rites
  Of gathering these Delights,   50
 And onely Sighs allows, till he
 Hath better Knitt, and spred Your Tree
  Where Union would last Long,
  Shee fixeth in the Young,
And so grows up. Great Spirits with more Love   55
Differre their Joyes, then Others doe them Prove.

But when Her Zone[2] shall come to be unty'd,
  And She be Twice Your Bride;
When Shee shall Blush, and straight waxe Pale, and then
  By turns doe Both agen;   60
 When Her owne Bashfullnesse shall prove
 The Second Nonage to Her Love;
  Then you will know what Blisse
  Angells both Have, and Misse;
 How Soules may[3] mixe, and take fresh growth,   65
 In Neither whole, and Whole in Both;
  Pleasures, that none can know,
  But such as have stayd so.
Wee from Long Loves at last to Hymen tend[4]
But Princes Fires beginne, where Subjects end.   70

  [1] *Yond*, Ed. 1651, C'.
  [2] *Tone*, Ed. 1651, corrected in *Errata* to *Zone*.
  [3] *do*, Ed. 1651, Ch.   [4] *send*, ibid.

TO PHILIP, EARL OF PEMBROKE, UPON HIS LORDSHIPS ELECTION OF CHANCELLOR OF THE UNIVERSITY OF OXFORD

My Lord,

When Studies now are blasted, and the times
Place us in false lights, and see Arts[1] as Crimes,
When to heape Knowledge is but thought to fil
The mind with more Advantage to doe ill:
When all your honoured Brothers choyce and store   5
Of Learn'd Remains with sweat and charge fetcht ore,
Are thought but uselesse peeces: and some trust
To see our Schooles mingled with Abby[2] dust,
That now you dare receive us, and professe
Your selfe our Patron, makes you come no lesse,   10
Then a new founder; whilst wee all allow
What was Defence before, is Building now.
And this you were reserv'd for, set apart
For times of hasard; as the Shield and Dart
Laid up in store to be extracted thence,   15
When serious need shall aske some try'd Defence;
And who more fit to manage the Gownes cause
Then you, whose even life may dare the Lawes,
And the Law-makers too: in whom the Great
Is twisted with the Good as Light with Heat;   20
What though your sadder cares doe not professe
To find the Circles squaring, or to guesse
How many sands within a grayne or two
Will fill the world, these speculations doe
Heale man from man; You'r he that can suggest   25
True rules, and fashion manners to the best:

[1] *Acts*, Ed. 1651, Ch.   [2] *Alby*, ibid.

You can preserve our Charters from the wrong
Of the untaught Towne, as farre as now the tongue
Doth from their understanding, You can give
Freedome to men, and make that freedome live; 30
And divert[1] hate from the now[2] hated Arts,
These are your great endowments, these your parts,
And 'tis our honest Boast, when this we scan
Wee give a Title, but receive a Man.

ON THE LADY NEWBURGH, WHO DYED
OF THE SMALL POX

I now believe that Heaven once shall shrink
Up like a shrivell'd Scrole, and what we think,
Spread like a larger Curtain, doth involve
The Worlds Great Fabrick, shall at length dissolve
Into a sparing Handfull, and to be   5
Only a Shrowd for its Mortality:
For her Disease Blest Soul, was but the same
Which alwaies raigneth in that upper Frame;
And hearing of her Fate, we boldly dare
Conclude that Stars, Sphears thicker Portions are   10
Only some Angry Pimples which foretell
That which at length must fall, now is not well.
  But why think we on Heav'n, when she is gone,
Almost as rich and fair a Mansion?
One who was good so young, that we from her   15
Against Philosophy may well infer
That Vertues are from Nature; that the Mind
Like the first Paradise may unrefind

[1] _divest_, Ch.   [2] _now from the_, Ed. 1651, Ch.

Boast Native Glories, and to Art not ow
That ought by Her it doth receive and show.   20
I may not call her Woman, for she ne'r
Study'd the Glass and Pencill, could not swear
Faith to the Lover, and when he was gone
The same unto the next, and yet keep none;
She could not draw ill Vapours like the Sun,   25
And drop them down upon some yonger One.
Alas her Mind was plac'd above these foul
Corruptions, still as high as now her Soul:
Nor had she any thought that e'r did fear
The open test of the Austerest Ear: 30
For all of them were such as wretches we
May wish, not hope, for this felicity,
That when we think on Heaven we may find
Thoughts, like the worst of hers, burn in our Mind.
   Let not the Ancient glory that they found   35
The Chain of Vertues, how they all were bound,
How met in one, we happier far did see
What they did either dream or Phophesie:
For since that she is gone, where can we find
A pair of Virtues met in all Mankind?   40
Someone perhaps is Chaste, Another Just,
A Third is valiant, but we may not trust
To see them throng'd again, but still alone
As in a Ring One Spark, one Pretious Stone.
I know some little Beauty, and one grain   45
Of any Vertue doth to Others gain
The Name of Saint or Goddess: but the Grace
Of every Limb in her, bright as the Face,
Presenting Chaster Beauties, did conspire
Only to stile her Woman: 'twas the fire   50

Of a religious mind that made her soar
So high above the Sex, her faith was more
Than others stumbling blindness; only here
She was Immodest, only bold to fear,
And thence adore: for She I must Confess   55
'Mongst all her Vertues had this one excess.
Forgive, thou all of goodness, if that I
By praising blemish, too much Majesty
Injures it self: where Art cannot express,
It veyls and leaves the rest unto a Guess.   60
So where weak Imitation failes, enshrowd
The awfull Deity in an envious Cloud;
Hadst thou not been so Good, so Vertuous,
Heaven had never been so Covetous;
Each parcell of thee must away, and we   65
Not have a Child left to resemble thee.
Nothing to shew thou wert, but what alone
Adds to our Brief, thy Ashes, or thy Stone:
And all our Glory can boast thus,
That we had one made Heaven Envy us;   70
I now begin to doubt whether it were
A true disease or no; We well may fear
We did mistake: The Gods whom they'l bereave
Do blindfold first, then plausibly deceive:
The Error's now found out, we are beguil'd,   75
Thou were Enammel'd rather than Defil'd.

AN EPITAPH ON MR POULTNEY

True to himself and Others, with whom both
Did bind alike a Promise and an Oath:
Free without Art, or Project; giving still

With no more Snare, or hope, than in his Will:
Whose mast'ring even Mind so ballanc'd all
His Thoughts, that they could neither rise nor fall:
Whose train'd desires ne'r tempted Simple Health
Taught not to vex but manage compos'd Wealth;
A season'd friend not tainted with Design,
Who made these words grow useless *Mine* and *Thine*; ɪ
An equall Master, whose sincere Intents
Ne'r chang'd good Servants to bad Instruments:
A constant Husband not divorc'd by Fate,
Loving, and Lov'd, happy in either State,
To whom the gratefull wife hath sadly drest   ɪ
One Monument here, Another in her Brest;
Poultney in both doth lye, who hitherto
To Others Liv'd, to himself only Now.

ON MISTRESS ABIGAIL LONG, WHO DYED
OF TWO IMPOSTUMES

So to a stronger guarded Fort we use
More Battring Engines Lest that death should loose
A nobler Conquest, Fates Conspiring come
Like Friendship payr'd into an Union.
     Tell me, you fatall Sisters, what rich Spoil,
What worthy Honour, is it to beguile
One Maid by two Fates? while you thus bereave
Of life, you do not conquer, but deceive:
Methinks an old decay'd and worn-out face,
A thing that once was Woman, and in Grace,   ɪ
One who each Night in Twenty Boxes lies
All took asunder: one w' hath sent her Eyes,

Her Nose, and Teeth, as Earnests unto Death,
Pawns to the Grave till she resign her Breath
And come her self, me thinks this Ruine might   15
Suffice and glut the Envy of your spight;
Why aime you at the Fair? must you have one
Whose every Limb doth shew perfection?
Whose well Compacted Members harmony
Speaks her to be Nature's Orthography?   20
Must she appear your Rage? why then farewell,
All, all the Vertue that on Earth did dwell.
Why do I call it Vertue? 'tis dishonour
Thus to bestow that Mortall little on her;
Something she had more Sacred, more Refin'd   25
Than Vertue is, something above the Mind
And low conceit of Man, something which Lame
Expression cannot reach, which wants a Name
'Cause 'twas ne'r known before; which I express
Fittest by leaving it unto a Guess;   30
She was that one, but to the Earth to shew
That Heavens Bounty did not only ow
Endowments unto Age, that Vertues were
Not to the Staff Confin'd, or the Gray-hair;
One that was fit ev'n in her Youth to be   35
An Hearer of the best Philosophy;
One that did teach by Carriage; One whose looks
Instructed more effectually than Books,
She was not taught like others how to place
A loose disordered Hair: the Comb and Glass,   40
As curious Trifles, rather made for loose
And wanton softness than for honest Use;
She did neglect: no Place left for the Checks
Of Careful Kindred: nothing but the Sex

Was womanish in her; she drest her Mind 45
As others do their Bodies, and refin'd
That better part with Care, and still did wear
More Jewels in her Manners than her Ear;
The World she past through, as the brighter Sun
Doth through unhallowed Stews and Brothels run, 50
Untouch'd, and uncorrupted; Sin she knew
As honest Men do Cheating, to eschew
Rather than practice; she might well have drest
All Minds, have dealt her Vertues to each Brest,
Enrich'd her Sex, and yet have still been one 55
Fit for the amazed Gods to gaze upon.

 Pardon, thou Soul of Goodness, if I wrong
Thine Ample Vertues with a sparing Tongue,
Alas, I am compell'd, speaking of thee,
To use one of thy Vertues, Modesty. 60

 Blest Virgin, but that very Name which cals
Thee blest into an Accusation fals;
Virgin is Imperfection, and we do
Conceive Increase to so much Beauty due;
And alas Beauty is no Phenix; why, 65
O why then wouldst thou not vouchsafe to try
Those Bonds of freedom, that when death did strike,
The World might shew, though not the same, the like.
Why wert not thou stamp'd in another Face,
That whom we now lament we might embrace? 70
That after thou hadst been long hid in Clay
Thou might'st appear fresh as the early Day,
And seem unto thy wondring kindred more
Young, although not more Vertuous than before?

 But I disturb thy Peace, sleep then among 75
Thy Ancestors deceas'd, who have been long

Lockt up in Silence, whom thy carefull Love
Doth visit in their Urns, as if thou'dst prove
Friendship in that forgetfull dust, and have
A Family united in the Grave   80
    Enjoy thy death, Blest Maid, nay further do
Enjoy that Name, that very little too;
Some use there is in Ill; we not repine
Or grudge at thy Disease; it did refine
Rather than kill; and thou art upwards gone,   85
Made purer even by Corruption.
    Whiles thus to Fate thou dost resign thy Breath,
    To thee a Birthday 'tis, to us a Death.

TO THE MEMORY OF THE MOST VERTUOUS MISTRESS URSULA SADLEIR, WHO DYED OF A FEAVER

      Thou whitest Soul, thou thine own Day,
      Not sully'd by the Bodies Clay,
          Fly to thy Native Seat,
          Surrounded with this Heat,
      Make thy Disease which would destroy thee   5
      Thy Charriot only to conveigh thee:
And while thou soar'st and leav'st us here beneath,
Wee'l think it thy translation, not thy death.

      But with this Empty feign'd Relief
      We do but flatter our Just Grief,   10
          And we as well may say
          That Martyr dy'd that day,
      Ride up in flames, whom we saw Burn,
      And into paler Ashes turn;

Who's he that such a Fate Translation calls
Where the whole Body like the Mantle falls?

But we beguile our Sorrows so
By a false scene of Specious Woe;
 Wee'l weigh, and count, and rate
 Our loss, then grieve the Fate.
Wee'l know the measure of her worth,
Then mete and deal our Sadness forth:
And when the Sum's made up, and all is clos'd,
Say Death undid what Love himself Compos'd.

What Morns did from her smiling rise?
What day was gather'd in her Eyes?
 What Air? What Truth? What Art?
 What Musick in each Part?
What Grace? what motion? and what skil?
How all by manage doubled still?
Thus 'twixt her self and Nature was a strife,
Nature Materials brought, but she the Life.

The Rose when't only pleas'd the Sence,
Arm'd with no Thorns to give Offence,
 That Rose, as yet Curse-free,
 Was not more mild than She,
Clear as the Tears that did bedew her,
Fresh as the Flowers that bestrew her,
Fair while She was, and when She was not, fair,
Some Ruines more than other Buildings are.

Gardens parch'd up with Heat do so
Her Fate as Fainter Emblems show.
 Thus Incense doth expire;
 Thus Perfumes dye in Fire;

Thus did Diana's Temple burn,   45
  And all her Shrines to Ashes turn.
As She a fairer Temple far did waste
She that was far more Goddess, and more Chaste.

  Returning thus as innocent
  To Heav'n as she to Earth was lent,   50
    Snatch'd hence ere she drank in
    The Taint of Age and Sin,
  Her Mind being yet a Paradise,
  Free from all weeds of spreading Vice,
We may Conclude her Feaver, without doubt   55
Was but the Flaming Sword to keep Eve out.

TO THE MEMORY OF THE MOST WORTHY
SIR HENRY SPELMAN

Though now the Times perhaps be such that nought
Was left thee but to dye, and 'twill be thought
An Exprobration to rehearse thy Deeds,
Thriving as Flowers among these courser weeds,
I cannot yet forbear to grieve, and tell   5
Thy skill to know, thy Valour to do well.
  And what can we do less, when thou art gone
Whose Tenents as thy Manners were thine own;
In not the same Times both the same; not mixt
With th' Ages Torrent, but still clear and Fixt;   10
As gentle Oyl upon the Streams doth glide
Not mingling with them, though it Smooth the Tide.
  What can we less, when thou art gone, whom we
Thought only so much living History?
Thou siftedst long hid Dust to find lost Ore   15

And searchedst Rubbish to encrease our Store.
Things of that Age thou shew'dst, that they seem'd new,
And stand admir'd as if they now first grew;
Time in thy learned Pages, as the Sun
On Ahaz Diall, does thus backward run.   20

Nor didst thou this affectedly, as they
Whom Humour leads to know out of the way.
Thy aym was Publike in't; thy Lamp and Night
Search'd untrod Paths only to set us right;
Thou didst consult the Ancients and their Writ,   25
To guard the Truth, not exercise the Wit;
Taking but what they said; not, as some do,
To find out what they may be wrested to;
Nor Hope, nor Faction, bought thy Mind to side,
Conscience depos'd all Parts, and was sole Guide.   30
So 'tis when Authors are not Slaves, but Men,
And do themselves maintain their own free Pen.

This 'twas that made the Priest in every Line,
This 'twas that made the Churches Cause be thine;
Who perhaps hence hath suffer'd the less wrong,   35
And owes thee much because sh'hath stood so long;
That though her Dress, her Discipline now faints,
Yet her Endowments fall not with her Saints.

This 'twas that made thee ransack all thy Store
To shew our Mother what she was before;   40
What Laws past, what Decrees; the where, and when
Her Tares were sow'n, and how pull'd up agen;
A body of that Building, and that Dress,
That Councels may Conspire and yet do less.

Nor doth late Practice take thee, but old Rights,   45
Witness that Charitable Piece that lights
Our Corps to unbought Graves, though Custome led

So against Nature, as to tax the dead.
Though use had made the Land oft purchas'd be,
And though oft purchas'd keep Propriety;   50
So that the well Prepared did yet fear,
Though not to dye, yet to undo the Heyr.

　　Had we what else thy Taper saw thee glean,
'Twould teach our Days perhaps a safer Mean;
Though what we see be much, it may be guess'd   55
As great was Shewn, so greater was suppress'd.

　　Go then, go up, Rich Soul; while we here grieve,
Climb till thou see what we do but believe;
W'have not time to rate thee; thy Fate's such,
We know we've lost; our Sons will say how much.   60

ON THE NATIVITY

For the King's Musick.

Omnes: 　Hark

1. 　　　　'Tis the Nuptiall Day of Heav'n and Earth;
2. 　　　　The Fathers Marriage, and the Sons blest Birth:
3. 　　　　The Spheres are giv'n us as a Ring; that Bliss,
　　　　　Which we call Grace is but the Deitie's kiss,
Ch.　　　And what we now do hear Blest Spirits sing, 5
　　　　　Is but the happy Po'sie of that Ring
1. 　　　　Whiles Glory thus takes Flesh, and th'Heavens
　　　　　　are bow'd
　　　　　May we not say God comes down in a Cloud?
2. 　　　　Peace dropping thus on Earth, Good will on Men,
　　　　　May we not say that Manna fals agen?   10
Ch.　　　All wonders we Confess are only his:
　　　　　But of these wonders, He the greatest is.

1. The Mother felt no pangs; for he did pass
As subtle Sun-beams do through purer Glass.
2. The Virgin no more loss of Name did find,   15
Than when her Vertues Issu'd from her Mind.
Ch. The Lilly of the Valleys thus did ow
Unto no Gard'ners Hands that he did grow.
1.   Blest Babe, thy Birth makes Heaven in the
Stall;
2. And we the Manger may thy Altar call: 20
3.   Thine and thy Mothers Eyes as Stars appear;
The Bull no Beast, but Constellation here.
Ch.   Thus Both were Born, the Gospell and the Law,
Moses in Flags did lye, thou in the Straw.
1.   Open, O Hearts,
These Gates lift up will win   25
2. The King of Glory here to enter in;
3. Flesh is his Veyl, and House: whiles thus we wooe,
The World will dwell among, and in us too.
Ch. Flesh is his Veyl, &c.

ON THE CIRCUMCISION

For the King's Musick.

1. Gently, O Gently, Father, do not bruise
That Tender Vine that hath no Branch to lose;
2. Be not too Cruel, see the Child doth Smile,
His Bloud was but his Mothers Milk erewhile,
1. *Lev.*   Fear not the pruning of your Vine,   5
Hee'l turn your Water into Wine;
2. *Lev.* The Mother's Milk that's now his Bloud,
Hereafter will become her Food.

Chor.	'Tis done; so doth the Balsam Tree endure
	The cruell Wounds of those whom it must Cure. 10
1. *Lev.*	'Tis but the Passions Essay: This young loss
	Only preludes unto his Riper Cross.
1.	Avert, good Heav'n, avert that Fate
	To so much Beauty so much Hate.
2. *Lev.*	Where so great Good is meant 15
	The Bloud's not lost, but spent.
Chor.	Thus Princes feel what People do amuse;
	The swelling's Ours, although the Lancing his
2.	When ye fair Heavens white Food bled,
	The Rose, say they, from thence grew Red. 20
	O then what more Miraculous good,
	Must spring from this diviner Floud?
2. *Lev.*	When that the Rose it self doth bleed,
	That Bloud will be the Churches Seed.
Chor.	When that the Rose, &c. 25

ON THE EPIPHANY

For the King's Musick.

1. *Mag.*	See this is He, whose Star
	Did becken us from far;
2. *Ma.*	And this the Mother whom the Heavens do
	Honour, and like Her, bring forth New Stars too.
3. *Ma.*	I know not which my Thoughts ought first
	admire: 5
	Here Shew, O Heav'n, another guiding fire.
Cho.	Alas, this Wonder's so above our Skill,
	That though w' have found him, we may seek him
	still.

1. *Ma.*   Since that our own are Silenc'd, This Mouth be
A more Inspired Oracle to me.   10
2. *Ma.*   And these Eyes be my Stars, my Light,
3. *Ma.*   And this Hand wash an Ethiop white.
Cho.   Wisdom Commands the Stars (we say)
But it was Ours thus to obey
1. *Ma.*   He makes our Gold seem Pebble stone;   15
2. *Ma.*   Sure 'tis their Greater Solomon;
1. *Ma.*   Our Myrrh and Frankinsence must not Contest;
3. *Ma.*   Diviner Perfumes breath from off her Breast.
2. *Ma.*   Blest Babe, receive our now disparag'd store.
3. *Ma.*   And where we cann't express, let us Adore.   20
Cho.   Who against Policy will hence convince,
That Land is blest, that hath so young a Prince.
To the King.   But as those Wise enrich'd his Stable, You
Great Soveraign, have enrich'd his Temple too,
The Sun by You hath not the Church beguil'd; 25
The Manger to the Altar's Reconcil'd:
Since then their Wisdom is by Yours out-gone,
Instead of Three Kings, Fame shall speak of One.
Cho.   Since then, &c.

THE QUEEN'S RETURN FROM THE
LOW COUNTRIES

Hallow the Threshold, Crown the Posts anew;
The day shall have its due:
Twist all our Victories into one bright wreath,
On which let Honour breath;
Then throw it round the Temples of our Queene;   5
'Tis Shee that must preserve those glories green.

When greater Tempests, then on Sea before,
     Receav'd Her on the shore,
When She was shot at, *for the King's own good*,
     By Villaines hir'd to Blood;   10
How bravely did Shee doe, how bravely Beare,
And shew'd, though they durst rage, Shee durst not feare.

Courage was cast about Her like a Dresse
     Of solemne Comelinesse;
A gather'd Mind, and an Untroubled Face   15
     Did give her dangers grace.
Thus arm'd with Innocence, secure they move,
Whose Highest Treason is but Highest Love.

As some Bright Starre, that runnes a direct[1] Course,
     Yet with Another's force,   20
Mixeth its vertue in a full dispence
     Of one joynt influence,
Such was Her mind to th'Kings, in all was done;
The Agents Diverse, but the Action One.

Look on Her Enemies, on their Godly Lyes,   25
     Their Holy Perjuries,
Their Curs'd encrease of much ill gotten wealth,
     By Rapine or by stealth.
Their crafty Friendships knit by equall guilt,
And the Crown-Martyrs blood so lately spilt.   30

Looke then upon Her selfe; Beauteous in Mind,
     Scarce Angells more refin'd;
Her actions Blancht, Her Conscience still Her Sway,
     And that not fearing Day:
Then you'll confesse Shee casts a double Beame,   35
Much shining by Her selfe, but none by Them.

    [1] *direct* in Ed. 1651, Cb., but *diverse* in *Epibat. Mar.*

Receive Her then as the new springing Light
  After a tedious Night:
As Holy Hermits do Revealed Truth;
  Or Æson did his youth.   40
Her presence is our Guard, our Strength, our Store;
The cold snatch some flames thence, the valiant more.

But something yet, our Holy Priests will say,
  Is wanting to the Day:
'Twere sinne to let so Blest a feast arise   45
  Without a Sacrifice.
True, if our Flocks were full. But being all
Are gone, the Many-headed Beast must fall.

THE DEATH OF THE RIGHT VALIANT
SIR BEVILL GRENVILL, KNIGHT

Not to be wrought by Malice, Gain, or Pride,
To a compliance with the Thriving Side;
Not to take Arms for love of Change, or Spight,
But only to maintain Afflicted Right;
Not to dye vainly in pursuit of Fame,   5
Perversely seeking after Voice and Name;
Is to Resolve, Fight, Dye, as Martyrs do:
And thus did He, Souldier, and Martyr too.
  He might (like some Reserved Men of State,
Who look not to the Cause, but to its Fate)   10
Have stood aloof, engag'd on Neither Side,
Prepar'd at last to strike in with the Tyde.
But well weigh'd Reason told him, that when Law
Either is Renounc'd, or Misapply'd by th'awe

Of false nam'd Common-wealths men;[1] when the Right 15
Of King, and Subject, is suppress'd by Might;
When all Religion either is Refus'd
As meer Pretence, or meerly, as That us'd;
When thus the Fury of Ambition Swells,
Who is not Active, Modestly Rebells.   20
Whence, in a just esteem, to Church and Crown
He offred All, and nothing thought his own.
This thrust Him into Action, Whole and Free,
Knowing no Interest but Loyalty;
Not loving Arms as Arms, or Strife for Strife;   25
Not Wastful, not yet Sparing of his Life;
A great Exactor of Himself, and then
By fair Commands no less of Other men;
Courage, and Judgment had their equall part,
Councell was added to a Generous Heart;   30
Affairs were justly tim'd; nor did he catch
At an Affected Fame of Quick Dispatch;
Things were Prepar'd, Debated, and then Done,
Nor rashly Brook[2], nor vainly Over-spun;
False Periods no where by Design were made,   35
As are by those, who make the Warr their Trade;
The Building still was suited to the Ground,
Whence every Action issu'd Full and Round.
We know who blind their Men with specious Lyes,
With Revelations, and with Prophecies,   40
Who promise two things to obtain a Third,
And are themselves by the like Motives stirr'd:
By no such Engines He His Souldiers[3] draws;
He knew no Arts, but Courage and the Cause;

---

[1] *Patriots, that*, Ed. 1651, Ch.
[2] *Broke*, ibid.   [3] *Shoulders*, Ch.

With these he brought them on, as well-train'd men, 45
And with these too[1] he brought them off agen.
I should, I know, track Him through all the Course
Of his great Actions, shew their worth and Force:
But, although all are Handsome, yet we cast
A more intentive Eye still on the last. 50
When now th'incensed Rebell[2] proudly came
Down, like a Torrent without Bank, or Damm;
When Undeserv'd Success urg'd on their force,
That Thunder must come down to stop their Course,
Or Granvill must step in; Then Granville stood, 55
And with Himself oppos'd, and checkt the Flood.
Conquest or Death, was all His Thought. So fire
Either orecomes, or doth it self expire.
His Courage work't like Flames, cast heat about,
Here, there, on this, on that side; None gave out; 60
Not any Pike in that Renowned Stand,
But took new Force from his Inspired[3] Hand;
Souldier encourag'd Souldier, Man urg'd Man.
And He urg'd All: so much Examples can.
Hurt upon Hurt, Wound upon Wound did call, 65
He was the But, the Mark, the Aim of All:
His Soul this while retir'd from Cell to Cell,
At last flew up from all, and then He fell:
But the Devoted Stand, enraged more
From that his Fate, ply'd hotter than before, 70
And Proud to fall with Him, sworn not to yield,
Each sought an Honour'd Grave, and[4] gain'd the Field.
Thus, He being fall'n, his Action fought a new:
And the Dead conquer'd, whiles the Living slew.

[1] *those two*, Ed. 1651, Ch. [2] *Legions*, ibid.
[3] *Inspiring*, ibid. [4] *so*, ibid.

This was not Natures Courage; nor that thing   75
We Valour call, which Time and Reason bring;
But a Diviner Fury, Fierce, and High,
Valour transported into Extasie.
Which Angells, looking on us from above,
Use to conveigh into the Souls they Love.   ,   80
[1]You now that boast the Spirit, and its sway,
Shew us his Second, and we'l give the Day.
We know your Politique Axiom—Lurk, or Fly.
Ye cannot Conquer, 'cause ye dare not Dye.
And though you thank God, that you lost none there, 85
Because th'were such, who Liv'd not when they were;
Yet your great Generalle (who doth Rise and Fall,
As his Successes do; whom you dare call,
As fame unto you doth Reports dispense,
Either a Traytor, or His Excellence)   90
How e'ere he reigns now by unheard of Laws,
Could wish His Fate together with his Cause.

    And Thou (Blest Soul) whose Clear Compacted Fame,
As Amber Bodies keeps, preserved thy Name,
Whose Life affords what doth content Both Eyes,   95
Glory for People, Substance for the Wise;
Go laden up with Spoyles, possess that Seat
To which the Valiant, when th'have done retreat:
And when thou seest an happy Period sent
To these Distractions, and the Storm quite spent;   100
Look down, and say: I have my share in All
Much good grew from my Life, Much from my Fall.

    [1] 12 ll. seq. omitted in Ed. 1651.

ON A VERTUOUS YOUNG GENTLEWOMAN
THAT DYED SUDDENLY

When the old flaming Prophet climb'd the sky
Who, at one Glympse, did vanish, and not dye
He made more Preface to a Death, than This,
So far from Sick, She did not breath amiss:
She who to Heaven more heaven doth annex,   5
Whose lowest Thought was above all our Sex,
Accounted nothing Death but t'be Repriv'd,
And dyed as free from sickness as she liv'd.
Others are dragg'd away, or must be driven,
She only saw her time and stept to Heaven;   10
Where Seraphimes view all her Glories o're
As one Return'd, that had been there before.
For while she did this Lower World adorn,
Her body seem'd rather assum'd than born;
So Rarifi'd, Advanc'd, so Pure and Whole,   15
That Body might have been another's Soul.
And equally a Miracle it were
That she could Dye, or that she could Live here.

THE DEATH OF THE MOST VERTUOUS GENTLE-
WOMAN, MISTRESS ASHFORD, WHO DYED IN
CHILD-BED

So when the great Elixar (which a Chast
And even Heat hath ripened) doth at last
Stand ready for the Birth, th'Alembick's womb
Not able to discharge, becomes its Tomb;

So that that studied stone is still Arts Cross,   5
Not known by it's Vertue so much as his Loss.
And we may think some envious Fates Combine
In that one Ounce to rob us of a Mine;
And can our Grief be less, whiles here we do
Lose not the Stone, but the Alembick too?   10
When Death Converts that hatching Heat to Cold,
And makes that Dust, which should make all else Gold.
 If Souls from Souls be kindled as some sing
That to be born and Light'ned is one Thing;
And that our life is but a tender Ray   15
Snatch'd by the Infant from the Mothers Day;
And if the Soul thus kindled must have been
The framer of the Body, the Souls Inn;
Our Loss is doubled then, for that young flame
Flowing from hers, must have been for the same,   20
As to have cast such Glories, shew'n such seeds,
Spread forth such matchless Vertues, done such deeds,
Moulded such beautious Limbs, that we might see
The Mother in each Grace, and think that she
Was but Reflected, whiles her Shape did pass   25
As the snatch'd likeness doth into the[1] Glass,
Which now in vain we look for, for our Streams
Of Light are but the Dawning of her Beams;
'Twas not her lot to lay up Deeds, and then
Twist them into one Vertue, as some Men   30
Do hoord up smaller gains, and when they grow
Up to a Sum, into one Purchase throw;
Her Mind came furnish'd in, did charg'd appear,
As Trees in the Creation, Vertues were
Meer Natures unto her; Nor did she know   35

[1] *a,* Ch.

Those signs of our defects, to bud and grow;
Goodness her Soul, not Action, was; and She
Found it the same to do well and to be;
So perfect that her speculations might
Have made her self the bound of her own sight; 40
And her Mind thus her Mind contemplating
In brief at once have been the Eye and thing.
Her Body was so pure that Nature might
Have broke it into Forms: That Buriall rite
Was here unfit, for it could not be said 45
"Earth unto Earth, Dust unto Dust was laid";
All being so simple that the quickest sight
Did judge her Limbs but so much fashion'd Light;
Her Eyes so beamy, you'ld have said the Sun
Lodg'd in those Orbs when that the Day was done; 50
Her Mouth that Treasure hid, that Pearls wer blots
And darkness, if Compar'd, no Gems but Spots.
Her Lips did like the Cherub's flames appear,
Set to keep off the bold for Coming there.
Her bosome such that you would guess 'twas this 55
Way that departed Souls pass'd to their Bliss.
Her Body thus perspicuous, and her Mind
So undefil'd, so Beautious, so Refin'd,
We may conclude the Lilly in the Glass
An Emblem, though a faint one, of her was. 60
What others now count qualities and Parts
She thought but Compliments, and meer By-Arts,
Yet did perform them with as perfect Grace
As they who do Arts among Vertues place.
She dancing in a cross perplexed thread 65
Could make such Labyrinths, that the guiding thread
Would be it self at loss, and yet you'ld swear

A Star mov'd not so Even in its Sphere;
No looser flames but Raptures came from thence,
Her Steps stirr'd Meditations up, and Sense   70
Resign'd delights to Reason, which were wrought
Not to Enchant the Eye, but catch the Thought.
    Had she but pleas'd to tune her Breath, the Winds
Would have been hush'd and listned, and those Minds
Whose Passions are their Blasts, would have been still, 75
As when the Halcyon sits: So that her skill
Gave Credit unto Fables, whiles we see,
Passions like Wilder Beasts thus tamed be.
Her very looks were tune, we might descry
Consort, and Judge of Musick by the Eye: 80
So that in Others that which we call Fair,
In her was Composition and good Air.
    When this I tell, will you not hence surmise
Death hath got leave to enter Paradise?
But why do I name Death? for as a Star   85
Which erewhile darted out a Light from far,
Shines not when neer the Brighter Sun; She thus
Is not extinct, but does lie hid to us.

NOVEMBER

or, Signal Dayes Observ'd in that Month in
relation to the Crown and Royal Family

Thou Sun that shed'st[1] the Day, look down and see
A Month more shining by Events than thee;
Departed Saints and Souls sign'd it before,
    But now the Living sign it more:

[1] *shewst*, later version.

Persons and Actions meet[1], all meant for Joy; 5
  But some build up, and some destroy;
Bate Us that Ushering Curse (so Dearly known)
  And then the Month is all our own;
So at the First, Darkness was thrown about
Th'unshapen Earth, and Light was then struck out. 10

Draw the first Curtain and the Scene is then
A Triple State of Cull'd and Trusted Men;
Men, in whose hands 'twas once to have given Us more
  Then our bold Fathers ask'd before;
Who had they us'd their Prince's Grace, had got 15
  What no Arms could, and Theirs will not:
What more than Witchcraft did our Blessing curse,
  And made the Cure make Evils worse.
'Tis the Third Day, throw in the Blackest Stone,
Mark it for Curs'd, and let it stand Alone. 20

But, hold! speak gentler things; this Fourth was seen
The softest Image of our Beauteous Queen:
Bring me a Lamb, not us'd to elder Food,
  That hath as yet more Milk than Blood;
That to the Honour of this early Bride 25
  (Like Thetis joyn'd[2] to Peleus side)
Some tender thing may fall: though none can be
  So White, so Tender, as is She[3]:
While we at home our little Turf debate,
She spreads our Glory to another State. 30

Next, View a Treason of the worst Intent,
Had not our own *done* more than Strangers *meant*:

---

[1] *met*, later version. See Note. [2] *come*, ibid.
[3] *So tender or so white as She*, ibid.

Religion is the Thing both sides pretend,
    But either to a different End;
They Covenant out of zeal to rear their own,   35
    These out of Zeal to pull all down:
Bless us from these, as them; but yet compare
    Those in the Vault, these in the Chair:
Though the just lot of unsuccessful Sin
Fix theirs without; you'l find worse heads within.   40

But, hark! what Thunder's that, and who those men
Flying towards Heaven, but soon fall down again?
Whose those black Corps cast on the Guilty Shore?
    'Tis Sin that swims to its own Dore;
'Tis the Third Scourge of Rebels, which allow'd   45
    Our Army, like the Prophets Cloud,
Did from a handfull rise, until at last
    By it their Sky was overcast:
But (as Snakes hiss after they've lost their Sting)
The Traytors call'd this Treachery in the King.   50

Away! and view the Graces and the Powers
Hov'ring aloof and dropping mingled Flowers
Upon a Cradle where an Infant lay
    More Grace, more Goddess than are they:
Thrice did they destine Her to pass the Seas;   55
    Love made her thrice to pass with Ease,
To raise a strength of Princes first, and then
    To raise another strength of men:
Most fruitful Queen, we boast both Gifts, and thus
The Day was meant to You, the joy to Us.   60

Next to this Mother stands a Virgin Queen,
Courting and Courted, wheresoever seen:

The People's love first from her Troubles grew;
    Her Reign then made that Love her due:
That Comely Order which did then adorn   6
    Both Fabrics, now by Faction's torn,
That Form by her allow'd of Common-Prayer
    Is stil'd vain beating of the Air:
How do they Honour, how Forsake her Crown,
Her Times are still cry'd up, but practis'd down.   7

Reach last the whitest Stone the World yet knew,
White as his Soul to whom the Day is due;
Son of the peaceful James, how is he blest
    With all his Blessings but his Rest!
Though undeserved Times call[1] all his Pow'rs,   7
    And Troubles season[2] other Hours;
Let this Day flow to Him, as void of care
    As Feasts to Godds and Poets are;
The Wish is Just, O Heavens, as[3] our strife
Hath added to his Care, adde Yee[4] to his Life.   8

And now since His large Heart with Hers is met,
Whose Day the Stars on purpose neare His[5] set;
NOVEMBER shall to me for ever shine
    Red in its Ink, redder in Wine:
And since the third Day (which hath now made shift 8
    T'absolve the Treasons of the Fift)
Cannot be well remember'd or forgot
    By Loyal Hearts, as if 'twere not:
The last Extream against the first We'll bring,
That gave us many Tyrants, this a KING.   9

---

[1] *cloud*, later version. See Note.   [2] *All troubles seize on*, ibid.
[3] *and*, ibid.   [4] *Yee*, omitted ibid.
[5] *neer have*, ibid.

CONFESSION

I do confess, O God, my wand'ring Fires
Are kindled not from Zeal, but loose desires;
  My ready Tears, shed from Instructed Eyes,
Have not been Pious Griefs, but Subtleties;
  And only sorry that Sins miss, I ow   5
To thwarted wishes al the Sighs I blow;
  My Fires thus merit Fire; my Tears the fall
Of Showers provoke; my Sighs for Blasts do call.
  O then Descend in Fire; but let it be
Such as snatch'd up the Prophet; such as We   10
Read of in Moses Bush, a Fire of Joy,
Sent to Enlighten, rather than Destroy.
  O then Descend in Showers; But let them be
Showers only and not Tempests; such as we
Feel from the Mornings Eye-lids; such as Feed,   15
Not Choak the sprouting of the Tender Seed.
  O then Descend in Blasts; But let them be
Blasts only, and not Whirlwinds; such as we
Take in for Health's sake, soft and easie Breaths,
Taught to Conveigh Refreshments, and not Deaths.   20
  So shall the Fury of my Fires asswage,
And that turn Fervour which was Brutish Rage;
  So shall my Tears be then untaught to feign,
And the diseased Waters Heal'd again;
  So shall my Sighs not be as Clouds t'invest   25
My Sins with Night, but Winds to purge my Breast.

SONGS FROM THE PLAYS

THE LADY ERRANT

THE PROLOGUE

Sacred to your Delight
Be the short Revels of this night;
That calme that in yond Myrtles moves,
    Crowne all your Thoughts, and Loves:
And as the fatall Yew-tree shews 5
No Spring among those happy Boughs,
So be all Care quite banisht hence
Whiles easie Quiet rocks your Sence.

We cannot here complain
Of want of Presence, or of Train; 10
For if choice Beauties make the Court,
    And their Light guild the Sport,
This honour'd Ring presents us here,
Glories as rich and fresh as there;
And it may under Question fall, 15
Which is more Court, This or White-Hall.

Be't so. But then the Face
Of what we bring fits not the Place,
And so we shall pull down what ere
    Your Glories have built here: 20
Yet if you will conceive that though
The Poem's forc'd, we are not so;

And that each Sex keeps to it's Part,
Nature may plead excuse for Art.

As then there's no Offence   25
Giv'n to the weak or Stubborn hence,
Being the Female's Habit is
    Her owne, and the Male's his:
So (if great things may steer by less)
May you the same in looks express: 30
Your weare is Smiles, and Gracious Eyes;
When ere you frown 'tis but disguise.

SONG

To carve our Loves in Myrtle rinds,
    And tell our Secrets to the Woods,
To send our Sighs by faithful Winds
    And trust our Tears unto the Flouds,
To call where no man hears,   5
And think that Rocks have Ears;
To Walke, and Rest, to Live and Dye,
And yet not know Whence, How, or Why;
To have our Hopes with Fears still checkt,
To credit Doubts, and Truth suspect,   10
    This, this is that we may
    A Lover's Absence say.
Follies without, are Cares within;
Where Eyes do fail, there Souls begin. (A. 1. S. 4)

VENUS FOR HER BELOV'D ADONIS

Wake my Adonis, do not dye;
One Life's enough for thee and I.
Where are thy words?[1] thy wiles?
Thy Loves[2], thy Frowns, thy smiles?

[1] *looks*, A. and D. 1669.   [2] *fears*, ibid.

Alas in vain I call;   5
One death hath snatch'd 'em all:
Yet Death's not deadly in that¹ Face,
Death in those Looks it self hath Grace.

'Twas this, 'twas this I feard
When thy pale Ghost appear'd;   10
This I presag'd when thund'ring Jove
Tore the best Myrtle in my Grove;
When my sick Rose-buds lost their smell,
And from my Temples untouch'd fell,
And 'Twas for some such thing   15
My Dove did hang² her wing.

Whither art thou my Deity gone?
Venus in Venus there is none.
In vain a Goddess now am I
Only to Grieve, and not to dye.   20
But I will love my Grief,
Make Tears my Tears relief;
And Sorrow shall to me
A new Adonis be.

And this no Fates can³ rob me of, whiles I   25
A Goddess am to Grieve, and⁴ not to Dye.

(A. III. S. 4)

PRIESTS SONG

1 *Priest.*   Apollo, who foretell'st what shall ensue,
              None speaks more Dark than thou, but none
              more true

---

¹ *thy*, P.B.   ² *first hung*, A. and D. 1669.
³ *the Fates shan't*, A. and D. 1669.   ⁴ *weep but*, P.B.

	If heard, Obscure; but yet if seen, most Bright,	
	Day's in thy Visage, in thy Sayings Night.	
Pr. Chor.	Day's, &c.	5
Lady.	Venus makes good what he Decrees,	
	And Love fulfils what he foresees,	
	Thus Gods help Gods, thus Mortals ow	
	Much to the Bayes, much to the Bow.	
La. Chor.	Much, &c.	10
Priest.	Phoebus at Present shewes us future things,	
	Our Trivets Counsell give, our Trees teach Kings,	
	And whilst our Oracle instructs the State,	
	Whate'r the Priest shall say the God makes Fate.	
Pr. Chor.	What e'r, &c.	15
Lady.	What are your Trivets to Love's wings?	
	They teach, but these do Conquer Kings:	
	Venus to Fate adds all the bliss,	
	She that makes Doves, makes Kingdoms kiss.	
La. Chor.	She that, &c.	20
La. & Pr.	Thus then the Myrtle and the Bayes we joyn,	
	And in one Wreath Wisdom and Love Combine.	

(A. v. S. 8)

THE EPILOGUE

Though we well know the Neighbouring Plain
Can strike from Reeds as high a Strain,
  And that the Scrip, and Crook
  May worst our Poet's Book;
Like Fayries yet we here could stay   5
Till Village Cocks proclaime the Day:

And whiles your Pleasure is the Theam,
    Feed and keep up the Dream.

But Sleep beginning now to shed
    Poppies on every Bed,   10
Love stay'd his hands, and said our Eyes
    This Night were made his Prize:
And now (instead of Poppies) flings
These wishes on you from his wings.

The Calm of Kingdoms new made Friends,   15
When both enjoy their Hopes, and Ends,
    The like in you Create,
    And make each Mind a State:
The thoughts of Princes, when they do
Meet Princes to coyn Princes too,   20
Possess your Breasts with Fire and Youth,
    And make each dream a Truth:
The Joyes of Friendship after Fight,
    Of Love's first happy Night,
Of Lords return'd, make you still greet,   25
    As when you first did meet.
And quilted thus from Grief and Fear,
Think you enjoy a Cyprus here.

THE ROYAL SLAVE

THE PROLOGUE TO THE KING AND QUEEN

From my Devotions yonder am I come,
Drawn by a neerer and more glorious Sun,
Hayle o ye sacred Lights; who doe inspire
    More than yond holy and eternall Fire.

A forreine Court lands here upon your shore,   5
  By shewing it's own worth to shew yours more:
Set here as Saphires are by your Queen's veines,
  Not to boast Colour, but confesse their· staynes.
No matter now for Art, you make all fit;
  Your Presence being still beyond all wit.   10
Whiles by such Majesty our Scene is drest,
You come both th'Entertainer, and the Guest.

THE PROLOGUE TO THE UNIVERSITY, AFTER THE KING'S DEPARTURE

After our Rites done to the King, we doe
  Think some Devotions to be paid to you.
But I could wish some Question hung up there,
That we by Genuine sounds might take your eare.
  Or that our Scene in Bodley's Building lay.   5
And th'Metaphysicks were cast into a Play.
  To please your Palats I could wish there were
A new Professour, Poet of the Chayre.
  But as where th'Earth cannot ascend, we[1] know
The Sun comes downe and cheers her here below.   10
  So we (the Stage being ayr'd now, and the Court
Not smelt) hope you'l descend unto our Sport;
And think it no great trespasse, if we doe
  Sinne o'r our Trifle once againe to you.
'Tis not the same as there, that glorious Prease   15
  Did passe both for the Matter, and the Dresse.
For where such Majesty was seen, we may
  Say, the Spectators only made the Play.

[1] *you*, Ed. 1651.

Expect no new thing yet; 'tis without doubt
   The former Face, only the Eyes put out.   20
But you add new ones to it, being sent
   As for our grace, so for our supplement.
We hope here's none inspired from late damn'd books
   Will sowre it into Tragedy with their looks;
The little Ruffe, or careless, without fear: 25
   May this securely see, securely hear:
There's no man shot at here, no Person's hit,
   All being as free from danger, as from wit.
And such should still the first adventures be
   Of him, who's but a Spy in Poetrie.   30
No Envy then or Faction feer we, where
   All like your selves is innocent and cleare.
The stage being private then, as none must sit,
   And, like a Trap, ley wait for sixpence wit;
So none must cry up Booty, or cry down;   35
   Such Mercenary Guise fits[1] not the Gown.
   No Traffique then: Applause or Hisse elsewhere
May pass as ware, 'tis only judgment here.

THE PROLOGUE TO THEIR MAJESTIES AT HAMPTON COURT

The Rites and Worship are both old, but you
Have pleas'd to make both Priest and People new.
The same Sun in yon Temple doth appear;
But th'are your Rayes, which give him lustre here.
That Fire hath watched e're since; but it hath been 5
Onely your gentler breath that Kept it in.

[1] *fit*, 2nd Ed. 1640.

Things of this nature scarce survive that night
That gives them Birth; they perish in the sight;
Cast by so far from after-life, that there
Is scarce ought can be said, but that they were.   10
Some influence may cross this fate; what You
Please to awaken must still come forth new.
And though the untouch'd Virgin Flow'r doth bring
The true and native Dowrys of the Spring;
Yet some desires there are perhaps, which do   15
Affect that Flower chas'd and sully'd too:
For in some bosomes stuck, it comes from thence
Double-perfum'd, and deeper strikes the Sense.
And we are bid plead this; fore seeing how
That which was fresh ere-while may languish now: 20
    Things twice seen loose; but when a King or Queen
Commands a second sight, they're then first seen.

THE PRIEST'S SONG

Come from the Dungeon to the Throne,
To be a King, and straight be none.
Reigne then awhile, that thou mayst be
Fitter to fall by Majesty.

Cho.   So beasts for Sacrifice we feed;   5
First they are crown'd, and then they bleed.

Wash with thy Bloud what wars have done
Offensive to our God the Sun:
That as thou fallest we may see
Him pleas'd and set as red as thee.   10
Enjoy the Gloryes then of state,
Whiles pleasures ripen thee for fate.

Cho.   So beasts, &c.   (A. 1. S. 2)

LOVE AND MUSICK[1]

Come my sweet, whiles every strane
   Calls our souls unto the Eare,
Where the greedy listning[2] fayne
    Would turn into the Sound they hear,
      Lest in desire   5
      To fill the Quire
      Themselves they tye
      To Harmony,
Let's Kiss and call them back againe.
Now let's orderly convcigh   10
   Our souls unto each other's Brest,
Where enterchanged let them stay
   Slumbering in a melting rest.
      Then with new fire
      Let them retire,   15
      And still present
      Sweet fresh content
Youthfull as the early[3] day.
Then let us a Tumult make,
   Shuffling[4] so our soules that we   20
Careless who did give or take,
    May not Know in whom they be:
      Then let each smother,
      And stifle the other,
      Till we expire   25
      In gentle fire
Scorning the forgetfull Lake.   (A. II. S. 3)

---

[1] Title given in A. and D. 1653.
[2] *listing*, Ed. 1651 and A. and D. 1653. The *Errata* in former corrects to *listening*.
[3] *earthly*, Marrow of Compliments.   [4] *suffering*, ibid.

SONG

1. Now, now, the Sun is fled
   Down into Tethy's[1] bed,
   Ceasing his solemne course awhile.
   What then?
2. 'Tis not to sleepe but be   5
   Merry all night, as we;
   Gods can be mad sometimes as well as men.

Cho   Then laugh we, and quaffe we, untill our rich noses
        Grow red and contest with our Chaplets of Roses.

1. If he be fled, whence may   10
   We have a second day,
   That shall not set till wee command?
2.   Here see.
   A day that does arise
   Like his, but with more eyes,   15
   And warmes us with a better fire than hee

Cho.   Then laugh we, &c.

1. 2.   Thus then wee chase the night
   With these true floods of light,
   This Lesbian wine, which with it's sparkling streams,
   Darting diviner Graces,   21
   Casts glories round our Faces,
   And dulls the Tapers with Majestique Beames.

Cho.   Then laugh we, &c.   (A. III. S. 1)

SONG

1. *Priest.*   Thou O bright Sun who seest all,
        Look down upon our Captives fall.
        Never was purer sacrifice:
        'Tis not a Man, but Vertue dyes.

---

[1] *Thetis*, Marrow of Compliments.

Cho.   While thus we pay our thanks propitious be,
      And grant us either Peace or Victory. 6

2. *Priest.* But thou O Sun may'st set, and then
      In brightnesse rise next morne agen,
      He, when he shall once leave this light,
      Will make and have eternal night. 10
Cho.   Good deeds may passe for Sacrifice, O than
      Accept the Vertues, and give back the Man

             (A. v. S. 7)

THE EPILOGUE TO THE KING AND QUEEN

Those glorious Triumphs of the Persian Court
Are honour'd much in being made your sport:
The Slave though freed by th'King, and his Priest too,
Thinks not his Pardon good, till seal'd by you:
And hopes, although his faults have many been, 5
To find here too the favour of a Queen.
For 'tis our forward duty that hath showne
These loyall faults in honour to your Throne.
Great joy doth bring some madnesse with it still;
Wee challenge that as title to do ill. 10
  Can you expect then perfect motion, where
'Tis the digression out of our spheare,
Which wheeles in this new course, t'expresse the sense
Of your approach, its best Intelligence?
O were you still fix'd to it! Your resort, 15
Makes us desire an everlasting Court:
And though we've read you o're so long, that we
Begin to Know each line of Majesty,

We think you snatch'd too soon, and grieve as they
Who for an half yeares night, part with their day.　　20
And shall, till you returne, though you appeare
In favours still, think darknesse in our Spheare.
Your sight will be preserv'd yet, though you rise:
When e're you goe, great Sir, hearts will have eyes.

THE EPILOGUE TO THE UNIVERSITY

　　Thus cited to a second night, we've here
　　Ventur'd our Errours to your weighing Eare.
We'd thought they'd have been dead, as soon as born;
For Dreams do seldom live untill the morn.
　　There's difference 'twixt a Colledge and a Court;　　5
The one expecteth Science, th'other sport.
Parts should be Dialogues there, but Poynts to you:
They look for pleasing, you for sound, and true.
We fear then we have injur'd those, whose Age
Doth make the Schools the measure of the Stage:　　10
And justly thence for want of Logicke darts,
May dread those sturdy Yeomen of the Arts.
　　We are not train'd yet to the Trade, none's fit
To fine for Poet, or for Player yet.
We hope you'l like it then, although rough fil'd;　　15
As the Nurse loves the lisping of the child.
　　The Slave (then truly Royall, if you shall
By your smiles too redeeme him from his fall)
Hopes you'l dismisse him so, that he may swear,
One Court being gone, he found another here.　　20
Though rais'd from slave to king, he vowes he will
Resume his former bonds, and be yours still.

THE EPILOGUE TO THEIR MAJESTIES
AT HAMPTON-COURT

The unfil'd Author, though he be assur'd,
That a bad Poet is a thing secur'd,
Fears yet he may miscarry, for some doe,
Having just nothing, lose that nothing too.
His comfort's yet, that though the Incense fly   5
Foule and unwelcome, and so scatter'd dye,
Neither the blot nor sin can on him stand,
Being the Censer's in Another hand.
For though the Peece be now mark'd his, and Known,
Yet the Repeaters make that Peece their own.   10
Being then a new Reciter some way is
Another Author, we are thus made his.
We therefore hope nothing shall here be seen
To make the Slave appeale from King or Queen:
From yourselves here, t'yourselves at Oxford; grace   15
And favour altring with the time and place,
So that some thence may deem it happy fell
There only, where you[1] meant to take all well.
'Tis then your Countenance that is the price
Must redeem this, and free the Captive twice.   20
He fears ill-fate the lesse, in that if you
Now Kill him, you Kill your own favour too.
    How e'er he will not 'gainst injustice cry;
    For you who made him live, may make him dye.

[1] *yee*, Ed. 1651.

THE ORDINARY

THE PROLOGUE

'Twould wrong our Author to bespeake your Eares;
Your Persons he adores, but Judgment feares:
For where you please but to dislike, he shall
Be Atheist thought, that worships not his Fall,
   Next to not marking 'tis his hope that you   5
Who can so ably judge, can pardon too.
His Conversation will not yet supply
Follies enough to make a Comedy;
He cannot write by th'Poll; nor Act we here
Scenes, which perhaps you should see liv'd elsewhere; 10
No guilty line traduceth any; all
We now present is but conjecturall;
'Tis a mere ghesse: Those then will be too blame,
Who make that Person, which he means but Name.
   That web of Manners which the Stage requires,   15
That masse of Humors which Poetique Fires
Take in, and boyle, and purge, and try, and then
With sublimated follies cheat those men
That first did vent them, are not yet his Art,
But as drown'd Islands, or the World's fifth Part   20
Lye undiscover'd; and he only Knows
Enough to make himself ridiculous.
   Think then, if here you find naught can delight,
   He hath not yet seen Vice enough to write.

     Saint Francis, and Saint Benedight,
     Blesse this house from wicked wight,
     From the Night mare and the Goblin,
     That is hight good fellow Robin.

Keep it from all evill Spirits,
Fayries, weezels, Rats and Ferrets,   30
    From Curfew time
    To the next prime.

LOVE ADMITS NO DELAY[1]

1. Come, O come, I brook no stay:
    He[2] doth not love that can delay—
      See how the stealing Night
      Hath blotted out the Light,
    And Tapers do supply the Day.   5

2. To be chaste is to be old,
    And that[3] foolish Girle that's cold
      Is fourscore at fifteen:
      Desires do write us green,
    And looser flames our youth unfold.   10

3. See the first Taper's almost gone[4],
    Thy flame like that will straight be none;
      And I as[5] it Expire
      Not able to hold fire.
    She loseth time that lies alone.   15

4. O[6] let us cherish then these Powr's
    Whiles we yet may call them ours:
      Then we best spend our time,
      When no dull zealous Chime
    But sprightfull Kisses strike the Hours.   20

                            (A. III. S. 3)

[1] Title in 1669 Edition.
[2] *She*, A. and D. 1669 and MS. Rawl.
[3] *the*, MS. Rawl.   [4] *done*, ibid.   [5] *like*, ibid.
[6] *Come*, ibid.

THE SONG OF THE ORDINARY CLUBBERS

Then our Musick is in Prime,
When our teeth keep triple time;
    Hungry Notes are fit for knels:
      May lankeness be
      No Quest to me.   5
    The Bagpipe sounds, when that it swels.

A Mooting Night brings wholesome smiles,
When John an Okes, and John a Stiles,
    Doe greaze the Lawyer's Satin.
      A Reading-Day   10
      Frights French away,
    The Benchers dare speak Latin.

He that's full doth Verse compose;
Hunger deals in sullen Prose:
    Take notice and Discard her.   15
      The empty Spit
      Ne'r cherish'd Wit,
    Minerva loves the Larder.

First to breakfast, then to dine,
Is to conquer Bellarmine: 20
    Distinctions then are budding.
      Old Sutcliff's Wit
      Did never hit,
    But after his Bag-pudding.   (A. iii. S. 5)

SONG

Whiles early light springs from the skies,
A fairer from your Bride doth rise;
A brighter day doth thence appear,
And make a second morning there:
      Her blush doth shed
      All o'r the bed,
      Clean shame-faced beames
      That spread in streames,
And purple round the modest aire.

I will not tell what shreeks, and cries,
What Angry Dishes, and what ties,
What pretty oaths then newly born
The listning Taper heard there sworn:
      Whiles froward she
      Most peevishly
      Did yielding fight
      To keep o'r night
What shee'd have profer'd you ere morn.

Faire, we know, maids do refuse
To grant what they do come to lose.
Intend a Conquest you that wed;
They would be chastly ravished.
      Not any kisse
      From Mrs Pris,
      If that you do
      Persuade and woe.
Know pleasure's by extorting fed.

O may her arms wax black and bleu
Only by hard encircling you:
May she round about you twine   30
Like the easie twisting Vine;
      And whiles you sip
      From her full lip
      Pleasures as new
      As morning Dew,   35
Let those soft Tyes your hearts combine.

                    (A. iv. S. 5)

SONG

Now thou our future Brother,
That shalt make this Spouse a Mother
     Spring up, and Dod's blessing on't.
Shew thy little sorrell Pate
And prove regenerate   5
     Before thou be brought to the Font.
May the Parish Surplice be
Cut in peeces quite for thee,
     To wrap thy soft body about;
So 'twill better service do   10
Reformed thus into
     The state of an Orthodox Clout.
When thou shalt leave the Cradle,
And shalt begin to waddle,
     And trudge in thy little Apron;   15
Mayst thou conceive a grace
Of half an hour's space,
     And rejoice in thy Friday Capon.

For an errour that's the Flocks
Name Mr Paul, but urge St Knoxe;   2c
   And at every reform'd Dinner,
Let cheese come in, and preaching,
And by that third Course teaching,
   Confirm an unsatisfi'd Sinner.
Thence grow up to hate a Ring,   2:
And defie an offering:
   And learn to sing what others say.
Let Christ-tide be thy fast,
And lent thy good repast:
   And regard not an Holy day.   3(

(A. IV. S. 5)

THE EPILOGUE

We have escap'd the Law, but yet do feare
Something that's harder answer'd, your sharp Eare.
O for a present slight now to beguile
That, and deceive you but of one good smile!
'Tis that must us; th'Author dares not look
For that good fortune to be sav'd by's Book.
To leave this blessed soyle is no great woe;
Our griefe's in leaving you, that make it so.
   For if you shall call in those Beames you lent,
   'Twould ev'n at Home create a Banishment.   I(

THE SIEDGE

THE DEDICATION TO THE KING

The first Draught of this Trifle was so ill,
That 'twas the Crime, not Issue of the Quill,

Shape being wanting, to avoid the shame
The Spunge was destin'd Critick, or the Flame;
My Mercy finding out this way alone   5
To mend it with one Blot, or make it none.
But touch'd with your Command, my Muse, like
    Steel
Kiss'd by the Loadstone, did new Motion feel;
Whence this redeem'd from Fire unto your Eye
(Only perhaps to perish Royally)   10
Fears 'tis no Pardon, but Reprivall, and ʾ
Dreads the same Fate, though from another Hand:
So that the Change but little comforteth;
Sentence from you being but the State of Death.
And that Fear comes from that Encrease of ill,   15
That the last Errours are the greatest still.
Th'are Errours yet commanded, and plead this,
That by Injunction they have done amisse.
Two Names are due to't then; and some may ghesse
That I obey, others that I transgresse: 20
The Prospect thus being Double-bounded, I
Hope that you'l put the first unto your eye;
That what th'extent of Light would stile offence,
The half-way stop may call Obedience.

CHORUS OF VIRGINS

. *Virg.* Strow we these Flowers as we goe,
       Which trod by thee will sweeter grow.
. *Virg.* Guard her, ye Pow'rs, if any be,
       That love afflicted Chastity.
. *Virg.* Her mind deserves a Princely Sway,   5
       But yet obtained another way.

2. *Virg.*   Her vertues fit her for a Throne,
           But of no choice, except her own.
1. *Virg.*   O then look down on his Desires,
           And either quench, or clense his Fires   10

                            (A. ii. S. 7)

TWO SONGS

Seal up her Eyes, O sleep, but flow
Mild, as her Manners, too and fro:
Slide soft into her, that yet shee
May receive no wound from thee.
And ye, present her thoughts, O Dreams,   5
With hushing winds, and purling streams
Whiles hovering silence sits without,
Carefull to keep disturbance out.
Thus seize her, Sleep, thus her again resign,
So what was Heavens gift, wee'l reckon thine. 10

                            (A. iii. S. 5)

See how the Emulous Gods do watch
Which of them first her Breath shall catch,
Ambitious to resign their Bliss,
Might they but feed on Aire like this.
Thus here protected she doth lie   5
Hedg'd with a Ring of Majesty.
And doth make Heaven all her own;
Never more safe, than when alone.
Thus whiles she sleeps Gods do descend and kiss.
They lend all other Breath, but borrow this. 10

                            (A. v. S. 3)

NOTES

Page 1

A PANEGYRIC TO THE MOST NOBLE LUCY,
COUNTESS OF CARLISLE.

Lady Lucy Percy, daughter of the 9th Earl of Northumberland,
married in 1617 James Hay, 1st Earl of Carlisle, then a widower.
Her husband died in March, 1636, and was famous for his extrava-
gant ways of living. "The charms and wit of his second wife, Lucy,
Countess of Carlisle, which were celebrated in verse by all the
poets of the day, including Carew, Cartwright, Herrick and Suckling,
and by Sir Toby Matthew in prose, made her a conspicuous figure
at the court of Charles 1" (Art. *Ency. Brit.*, "Carlisle"). Cartwright
here duly pays his devotion to "Lucinda's sacred shrine."

18. *Monograms*: probably meaning the preliminary sketch or
outline of a picture. Ben Jonson uses the word in this learned
sense (*Underwoods, Poet to Painter*):

> You were not tied by any painter's law
> To square my circle, I confess, but draw
> My superficies : that was all you saw.
> Which if in compass of no art it came
> To be described by a monogram,
> With one great blot you had formed me as I am.

See the article on "Monogram" in the *New English Dictionary*.
'Cicero attributes to Epicurus the use of this word (applied with
the virtual sense 'unsubstantial') as descriptive of the gods according
to his conception of them, and Lucilius uses *ni mogrammus* for a
thin and colourless person, a 'mere shadow.' Nonius (*c.* 280), who
has preserved the passage of Lucilius, explains the word as designating
a picture drawn in line only, before the colour is applied."

The *monogram* sometimes refers to the mystic Christian symbol
of the Cross, and so might in this sense be compared with the temple.

33. *Amber Boxes*: boxes of ambergris, sweet perfume.

65. *And when We Men, th' weaker Vessels*: the irony is lost
in the present century. Compare Cartwright's remarks in his
Lady Errant, opening lines:

> And if you see not Women plead, and judge,
> Raise, and depress, reward and punish, carry
> Things how they please, and turn the Politique Door
> Upon new hindges very shortly, never
> Believe the Oracle.

70. *tinctures*: i.e. colours; the tincture, in the singular, was the great elixir sought by the alchemists.

109. *Ingerite*: innate, a rare word.

115. *your Father's glorious Name*: Henry Percy, 9th Earl o Northumberland (1564–1632), was imprisoned for sixteen years in the Tower. He engaged himself there in scientific and literary work, and his daughter Lucy was with him for some years.

119. *th' Elixar*: i.e. the ideal *elixir vitae* of the alchemists, which was to vanquish death. But the word was often used, and indeed, possibly here, as an equivalent to "quintessence." Cf. Donne

> But I am by her death (which word wrongs her)
> Of the first nothing, the Elixer grown...,

and v. Prof. Grierson's note in his edition of Donne (Vol. II, p. 38) Cartwright is too fond of the word. In the poem to Mrs Ashford he remarks truly, "That studied Stone is still Art's Cross."

123. *your Valorous Brother*: Algernon Percy, 10th Earl o Northumberland (1602–1668), was created (1638) Lord High Admira of England. He is famous for no particular sea victories, but trie to remedy many abuses in naval affairs. He was in command o the fleet for the Parliament during the Civil War.

Page 6

ON THE IMPERFECTION OF CHRIST CHURCH BUILDINGS

There is a MS. text of this poem in the British Museum (Add MSS. 22602, f. 20 b). In MS. Rawl. 696 (Bodl.) there is a collection of select passages from Cartwright's plays and poems. From this poem, for example, is chosen:

> Ruins here stand ruins as if none
> Dearst be so bold as once to cast a stone.
> . . . .
> Nor our windows may for Doctrine passe
> And we as (Paule) see misteryes in a glasse.
> We know that he who in the mount did give
> Those laws by which the people were to live,
> If they had needed them as now they doe
> Would have bestow'd the Stone for Tables too.

Christ Church "has of late years been much beautified by Bryar Duppa and Samuel Fell, Deans, who also built the fine porch and Stayr-Case to the hall anno 1630. Nevertheless the Roof of the northern and part of the western Square were not covered til after ye Restoration of the King, but lay exposed to ye injury o all kinds of weather." (*Account f Oxford*, by Thos. Baskerville. c. 1670–1700.)

14. *When 'twill be thought no College, but a Quar*: Quar is still used in Gloucestershire and west country dialects for "quarry." The word occurs a good deal in contemporary work: frequently, for example, in the *Du Bartas* of Joshua Sylvester.

35. *Escheated*: here used in the wider sense of "confiscated" or "forfeited."

41. *Two sacred things were thought (by judging souls)*
     Beyond the Kingdomes Pow'r, Christchurch and Pauls,
     Till, by a Light from Heaven shewn, the one
     Did gain his second Renovation.

In 1561 the spire of St Paul's was struck and destroyed by lightning. Inigo Jones carried out some subsequent renovation work. Waller has a poem "On the repairing of St Pauls" (1633). But the great fire in 1666 postponed the work, and it was not until 1675 that the foundation stone of the new building was laid.

Renovation is to be pronounced as of five syllables; endings in -science, -ion, or in -ation are pronounced as dissyllabic or trisyllabic, though only at the end of a line. Cartwright is fond of this use of the syllables: it becomes, in his case, a mannerism. So, for example, in the following:

> I send my (Muse) to one that knows
> What each Relation ows,
> One who keeps waking in his Breast
> No other sense
> But Conscience,
> That only is his Interest.

Here the ending of "Relation" is normal, while that of "Conscience" is dissyllabic. Again in *A Panegyric to the...Countesse of Carlisl*, l. 145, we have

> Hail your own Glass and Object, who alone
> Deserve to see your Own Reflection.

Page 8

A CONTINUATION OF THE SAME TO THE PRINCE OF WALES.

Charles II was born in 1630, and Duppa became his tutor in 1634.

20. *The Eldest Tear of Balsam*: where "balsam" is made to stand for the *tree* from which the healing juice is extracted. So Jeremy Taylor writes in one of his sermons, of the

"tears of the balsam of Judea."

25. *An Act, to which some could not well arive*
     After their fifty, done by you at five.
The lines enable us to fix the date of the poem as 1635.

27. *Nephews*: meaning, of course, grandchildren or descendants.

30. *All better Vertues now are call'd the Prince*: This is the "Cartwright style" in all its naïve excellence.

Page 10

ON HIS MAJESTY'S RECOVERY FROM THE
SMALL POX, 1633.

This poem is No. 94 in the *Pro Rege suo Soteria* where there is
also a Latin poem by Cartwright. Cartwright's contributions
to these University collections are all noticed together in the Introduction. The occasion of this particular poem, seems, according
to Madan, to have been "an illness of the king (variolae, scarlet
fever?) late in 1632." The malady, at any rate, was scarcely
serious.

Page 11

ON H.M.'S RETURN FROM SCOTLAND.

No 118 in the *Solis Britannici Perigaeum* (1633). The perigee
of the sun is its position nearest to the earth. No. 34 in the same
collection is a Latin poem by Cartwright. Duppa's contribution
(No. 116) makes a new beginning in the series, and the subsequent
poems are addressed to the Queen. Charles I visited Edinburgh
in 1633 to be crowned.

9.   *When the quill*
     Ceaseth to strike, the string yet trembles still.

Quill here stands for the plectrum made from the quill of a feather.

30.   *Their eager love, and Loyalty:* Cartwright shows his own
eager loyalty, for Charles's visit to Scotland comprised a long series
of diplomatic mistakes, chiefly in regard to religious policy; even
his coronation was carried out in the manner most likely to upset
Scottish prejudice.

Page 13

TO THE QUEEN ON THE SAME OCCASION.

10.   *parcell:* both the modern senses of the word were equally
in use in the 17th century. Cf. *Lady Powlet,* l. 25:

     Each Parcell so expressive, and so fit,
     That the whole seems not so much wrought, as writ.

Page 14

ON THE BIRTH OF THE DUKE OF YORK.

No. 106 in the *Vitis Carminae Gemma Altera.* (Ox. 1633.)
Cartwright's Latin contribution is No. 27. The Duke of York,
afterwards James II, was born Oct. 13, 1633.

43.   *Yet if hereafter unfil'd people shall:* Cartwright uses the
word *unfil'd* more than once. Jonson, he says, did not over-do
the application of the *"file"* to his poetry. He refers to himself
(3rd Epilogue to *The Royal Slave*) as an "unfil'd Author." The verb
"to file" as an equivalent of "to polish" in a literary sense was
used by the ancients, and applied technically of poetic craftsmanship, by many old authors, Skelton, Wither, Ben Jonson and

Dryden amongst others. The old enchanter in *The Faerie Queene* (1, i, 35) "well could file his tongue as smooth as glas." But in the actual case annotated the word has the general sense "uncultured."

56.   *These faire unspotted Volumes, when she views*
        In Him that glance, in Her that decent grace.

The "Her" was Mary, afterwards princess of Orange, born Nov. 4th, 1631.

Page 16

TO DR DUPPA.

Duppa (1588–1662) was educated at Westminster and was afterwards student of Christ Church, Oxford. He became chaplain to the Earl of Dorset, was on friendly terms with the Duke of Buckingham, and in 1629 was appointed Dean of Christ Church. He was Vice-Chancellor 1632 and 1633, in 1634 Chancellor of Salisbury, then tutor to the Prince of Wales and Duke of Gloucester; in 1638 Bishop of Chichester, in 1641 of Salisbury, and finally in 1660 of Winchester.

This poem was probably written directly after Duppa's appointment as royal tutor.

28.   Duppa remained Dean of Christ Church until 1638.

Page 19

TO THE SAME IMMEDIATELY AFTER THE PUBLICK ACT AT OXON, 1634.

For an account of the celebration of "the Publick Act," see Evelyn's *Diary* for July 8th, 1654. The day, he says, "was spent in hearing several exercises in the schools; and, after dinner, the Proctor opened the Act at St Mary's according to custom, and the Prevaricators, their drollery....10th, in the afternoon tarried out the whole Act in St Mary's, the long speeches of the Proctors, the Vice-Chancellor, the several professors, creation of Doctors by the cap, ring, kiss, etc., those ancient ceremonies and institutions as yet not wholly abolished..." (And see also *ibid.* 1669, July 10.)

21.   *Where (in my Judgement) the best thing to see*
        Had bee jerusalem or Nineveh,
        Where, for true Exercise, none could surpass
        The Puppets, and Great Britaines Looking Glas.

A Looking Glass for London and England is the title of a play written about 1594 by Greene and Lodge, where the Old Testament story of Nineveh is held up, by way of mirror and example, to London. Nineveh was evidently one of the most popular of the old puppet shows. "Jerusalem," says Lanthorn Leatherhead, the puppet showman in *Bartholmew Fair* (v, i). "was a stately thing, and so was Nineveh, and the City of Norwich, and Sodom and Gomorrah...but the Gunpowder Plot, there was a get-penny." Cowley in his play *Cutter of Coleman Street* (v, ii) speaks of "the Widow, who ne'er saw any Shew yet, but the Puppet-play of Nineve."

37. *That do no questions relish but what be
Bord'ring upon the Absolute Decree.*

Cartwright is referring to one of the most commonly used of the
theological terms in the long-continued debate between the Calvinist
and Armenian positions in the church. The "decree" of God, said
Arminius, is "absolute" with regard to His own actions, but only
conditional with regard to man's. Prynne in *Anti-Arminianisme*
(1630) declared that the doctrine of his opponents "makes man an
absolute, an independent creature." "Venting reprobation" again
implies the Calvinistic teaching of predestination.

41. *Give me the sight
Of the Lay Exercise on Monday night.*

Evelyn speaks of the "magnificent entertainment at Wadham Hall"
which he attended on a similar occasion.

52. *Christian Freedom*: an expression often found on the lips
of Puritans. See the note on "Christian Liberty," *The Chambermaid's Posset*, p. 188, l. 39.

60. *No brother then known by the rowling White*: So in the song
of Cocklorrel:

> His stomach was queasy...
> To help it he called for a puritan poacht,
> That used to turn up the eggs of his eyes;

and in *The Chambermaid's Posset* (l. 61) referred to above:

> The Pig that for haste, much like a Devout
> Entranced Brother, was wont to come in
> With white staring Eyes...

63. *My Lords fee-buck closeth bothe Eyes and Eares*: The word
"fee-buck" is extremely rare. It occurs in a passage in Cartwright's
play *The Siedge* (iv, ii): "pay your debts with Countenance; Put
off your Mercer with your Fee buck for that Season," and so forth.
The *New English Dictionary* gives the meaning "? a buck received
as a perquisite," but appends no other instance.

The best comment on its meaning that I know occurs in some
lines from Dryden's *Satire on the Dutch* (1662):

> As needy gallants, in the scrivener's hands,
> Court the rich knaves that gripe their mortgaged lands;
> The first fat buck of all the season's sent,
> And keeper takes no fee in compliment;
> The dotage of some Englishmen is such,
> To fawn on those who ruin them—the Dutch.

The first buck of the season, shot by keeper or tenant or whomsoever,
is the perquisite of the landlord, who, however, is expected, in
courtesy, to make some return. But the "Courtier turn'd Captain"
in *The Siedge* and the "needy gallant" of Dryden make a curious
coincidence. It may have been used later to mean any kind of
present made to ward off foreclosure. Compare Hall's *Satires*,
Book v. There is a passage, interesting on this account, in *The
Bride of Lammermoor* (Chapter iii). The forester is speaking:

"It was a disheartening thing when none of the gentles came down to see the sport...It was not so, he had heard, in Lord Ravenswood's time: when a buck was to be killed, man and mother's son ran to see; and when the deer fell, the knife was always presented to the knight, and he never gave less than a dollar for the compliment."

68. *Minshew*, who flourished about 1617, was a famous lexicographer. He published several dictionaries, and was a friend of Sir Henry Spelman, to whose memory Cartwright dedicated one of his poems.

70. *that wiser Statute*: The statutes of the University had been undergoing revision for some time. A book containing the new rules was published during Dr Duppa's Vice-Chancellorship, on the 22nd July, 1634. These statutes were distasteful to the Anti-Arminians (v. Wood, *Antiq*. I, 390 et seq.): "Statutum est, quod qui ad Doctoratum in S. Theologia aspirat, post susceptum Baccalaurei in Theologia Gradum, per quatuor Annos integros publicum Theologiae Praelectorem audiat, priusquam ad Incipiendum in eadem Facultate admittatur."

Page 21
ON THE GREAT FROST.

Cf. *Diary* of Archbishop Laud. *Dec.* 10, 1634. "That night the frost began, the Thames almost frozen; and it continued until the Sunday, sevennight after...Jan, 5. Monday night being Twelfth Eve, the frost began again; the Thames was frozen over, and continued so till Feb. 3." A MS. Version of this poem exists in the Malone collection in the Bodleian (21).

51. *We laugh at fire-briefs now, although they be*
    Commended to us by His Majesty.

"A fire-brief was a circular letter asking for assistance for sufferers by fire." No other reference is given by the *N.E.D.*

60. *Bowker* appears to have been one of the superior prognosticators. He had in fact prophesied "much snow, fierce winds, hard frost" for December. However, he says, "It is sufficient for an Artist though he attaine not the End, always to performe so much as the rules of Art require, which our common Almanacke-writers never do."

65. *We now think Alabaster true, and look*
    A sudden Trump should antedate his Book.

Alabaster (1567–1640), noted for his Latin poetry, wrote also mystical and cabalistic books. *Ecce Sponsus Venit* concerns the end of the world.

Page 24
TO THE LADY PAWLETT.

A series of these poems in MS. were presented to her in Convocation on July 9th, 1636 (v. Macray, *Annals of the Bodleien*, p. 65, note). There is another note also to this effect by F. Madan in the collection in the Bodleian (*MSS. Bodl. 22*). Cartwright's poem is the first, and the other contributions are by less known men, students of New College. "A curious piece of needlework," perhaps the identical one, was formerly No. 346 on the list of curiosities kept in the Anatomy School at Oxford.

The Lady Elizabeth is to be distinguished from the Lady Jane Pawlett, who died in 1631 and was also a lady of very pious disposition. In the edition of Ben Jonson's works with Gifford's notes (ed. Cunningham, 1910, Vol. III, p. 354, note) this confusion is made, and Cartwright's poem instanced as one addressed to the Lady Jane. Besides Ben Jonson, both Milton and Sir J. Beaumont have written elegiac poems to the latter lady, first wife of John Pawlett, fifth Marquis of Winchester. The Lady Elizabeth was either the second wife of John Pawlett[1], and daughter of Christopher Ken of Somerset, or a daughter of the third Marquis.

There is a version of this poem in the *Parnassus Biceps* (1656).

26. *That the whole seems not so much wrought, as writ*: "Wrought" was sometimes used for the past participle of "write." Compare Donne's poem *To Mr R. W.* (l. 11):

> Wright then, that my griefes which thine got may bee
> Cured by thy charming soveraigne melodee,

and see the note thereon by Grierson in his edition of Donne's *Poetical Works*, Vol. II, p. 168.

Page 26

TO MR W. B. AT THE BIRTH OF HIS FIRST CHILD.

W. B. might be William Backhouse, the Rosicrucian philosopher (1593–1662), who studied at Christ Church, and had two sons. Will Burton, the antiquary (1609–57), *not* the elder brother of Robert, was compelled to leave Oxford in 1630 on account of indigence.

Cf. l. 36:

> I wish him...
> His Fathers learning, but more wealth.

Page 28

FOR A YOUNG LORD TO HIS MISTRESS, WHO HAD TAUGHT HIM A SONG.

This is also quoted in full by *The Retrospective Review*.

15, 16. *As when a gentle Evening Showre*
Calls forth, and adds, Sent to the Flower.

Cf. *To the Queen*, 1633, l. 15, p. 13:

> As when in thirsty flowers, a gentle dew
> Awakes the sent which slept, not gives a new.

---

[1] Died 1649.

Page 29

ON MR STOKES.

The Vaulting Master : or, The Art of Vaulting...Now primarily set forth by Will: Stokes, printed Oxford, 1652. This is the earliest edition in the British Museum, but there was an earlier edition printed in London in 1641, of which there is a copy in the library of Worcester College, Oxford. See Evelyn, 1638. *22nd Jan.* "I would needs be admitted into the dancing and vaulting schools, of which late activity one Stokes, the master, did afterwards set forth a pretty book, which was published, with many witty Elogies before it." The present text is from the MS. 178 (Malone 21) in the Bodleian, for neither the 1641 nor the 1652 edition contains any commendatory poem by Cartwright. *Ephialtes* I take to mean flying- or night-mare.

3. *Rooke*: in the old disparaging sense, applied to persons.

10. *His tricks are here in figures dimme.* Each particular vaulting exercise, the *Pomado*, *Strapado*, *Herculean leap* and so forth, is illustrated in the original editions by a rough woodcut. In *Cynthia's Revels*, Hedon, "a gallant wholly consecrated to his pleasure," "courts ladies with how many great horse he hath rid that morning, or how oft he hath done the whole, or half the pommado in a seven-night before."

13.   *Were Dee alive, or Billingsley,*
       We shortly should each passage see
       Demonstrated by A.B.C.

John Dee (1527–1608) was the great mathematician and famous sorcerer in the time of Queen Elizabeth. Sir Henry Billingsley, Lord Mayor of London, who died in 1606, first translated Euclid into English.

25. *Vectures* are "carriages" or positions.

56. *Sheen*, referring to the royal mews there. One or two of these topical references are obscure. Who is Tom Charles?

61. *Theutobocchus.* A marginal note in all the 1651 editions, which I have seen, gives [Florus : "Lib. 3. c. 3." The incident is thus related : "Certe rex ipse Theutobocchus quaternos, senosque equos transilire solitus, vix unum, quum fugeret, ascendit, proximoque in saltu comprehensus, insigne spectaculum triumphi fuit" (III, iii, 10).

71.   *By Jove 'tis thou must Leap, or mit,*
       To pull bright honour from the Moon.

Says Hotspur in 1 *Henry IV.* I, iii, 201 :

       By Heaven, methinks it were an easy leap
       To pluck bright honour from the pale-fac'd moon.

Cartwright does not disdain the imaginative ideas of "dull" Shakespeare.

Page 32

ON ONE WEEPING.

The best text of this poem is from the Malone MSS. No. 21 in the Bodleian. *The Teares*, which is the corresponding poem in the 1651 edn., contains only fourteen lines, most of which occur in the longer, and apparently earlier poem. *The Teares* as given in the 1651 edn. is as follows (cf. the text of *On One Weeping*):

> *If Souls consist of water I*
> *May swear yours glides out of your Eye :*
> If they may wounds receive, and prove
> Festered through Grief, or ancient Love,
> Then Fairest, through these Christall doores
> Tears flow as purgings of your Sores.
> *And now the certain Cause I know*
> *Whence the Rose and Lilly grow.*
> *In your fair Cheeks, The often showers*
> *Which you thus weep, to breed these flowers.*
> *If that the Flouds could Venus bring*
> *And warlike Mars from Flowers spring.*
> *Why may not hence two Gods arise*
> *This from your Cheeks, that from your eyes ?*

5. *easy-tutour'd eye*: *tutoured* is a word Cartwright is very fond of using; cf. e.g. *Falsehood*, Stanza IV, "A tutour'd oath," and *Confession*, l. 3, "My ready Tears, shed from Instructed Eyes."

25. *O now the certaine cause I knowe*
From whence the rose and Lilly grow.

These and the following six lines are set to music in Lawes' *Ayres and Dialogues*, Book I. They are so quoted also in *The Retrospective Review*, where the poem is described as one of the "few pretty gems" of the volume. Cf. Strode's poem, *A Lover to his Mistress*:

> I'll tell you how the Rose did first grow redde.

Many are the ways in which "the goodly hue of white and red with which the cheeks are sprinkled" has been painted, and the idea of the lily and the rose has become a commonplace of poetry. It is found in Thomas Watson's "correct" description of the ideal fair lady, when he "praiseth the person and beautifull ornamentes of his love as they lie in order." So in Spenser's minute description of Belphoebe (*Faerie Queene*, II, iii, 25):

> And in her cheekes the vermeil red did shew
> Like roses in a bed of lilies shed.

Sidney's

> Where roses gules are borne in silver field

(*Astrophel and Stella*, XIV) is carried on by Drummond (*Poems*, Song I) to

> Her either cheek resembl'd a blushing morn
> Or roses gules in field of lilies borne.

Cartwright was probably thinking of something more recent. Geo. Sandys versified the *Song of Solomon* in English (published in 1641), and translated chapter five, verse ten—where the English prose rendering has

My beloved is white and ruddy—

to the following couplet

Lo! in his face the blushing rose
Join'd with the virgin lily grows.

Both Strode and Cartwright appear to have noticed, and applied to their own ends, the ingenuity of the paraphrase.

Page 34

A SONG OF DALLIANCE.

This poem has been recently printed by Mr A. H. Bullen in his *Speculum Amantis* (1889). My text here is taken from *Sportive Wit: The Muses merriment* (1656) in the Bodleian Library, where it is headed "Cartwright's Song of Dalliance. Never printed before." Mr Bullen thinks it "unquestionably the finest of Cartwright's poems" and calls it "magnificent." Another version (*Love's Courtship*) is to be found in *Parnassus Biceps* (1656). The variant readings will be found in the footnotes to the poem.

Page 35

PARCHMENT.

1. *Plain Shepherd's attire was only Gray*: so Greene in *Friar Bacon and Friar Bungay* (III, 119):

Proportion'd as was Paris, when, in grey,
He courted Œnon in the vale by Troy.

FALSEHOOD.

One of the most living of Cartwright's pieces; it was interesting to see the first two verses of the poem quoted recently in a London daily paper (*Daily Mirror*, May 21st, 1912). Corser (*Collectanea*) quotes all but the last two stanzas.

Page 37

BEAUTY AND DENIALL.

17. *But O we scorn the prefer'd Lip and Face*: this and the following seven lines are quoted in *The Retrospective Review*.

Page 39

TO CUPID.

Set to music by Lawes (v. *Ayres and Dialogues*, Book II, 1665). It is there called *A Prayer to Cupid*. Lawes' version is followed by Corser.

Page 40

A SIGH.

1. *I sent a Sigh unto my Blest one's Eare,*
  Which lost it's way, and never did come there.

Cf. *Absence*:

  Fly, O fly sad Sigh, and bear
  These few Words into his Ear.

A COMPLAINT AGAINST CUPID.

This poem is also quoted by Corser.

Page 41

SADNESS.

Quoted in full by *The Retrospective Review.*

Page 43.

TO THE MEMORY OF A SHIPWRECKED VIRGIN.

Quoted by *The Retrospective Review* as a specimen of Cartwright's "fanciful and perhaps somewhat conceited style." The first few lines are certainly "somewhat conceited."

Page 45

TO A PAINTER'S HANDSOME DAUGHTER.

Printed in *Parnassus Biceps* (1656).

4. *draughts*: cf. Bacon, *Advancement of Learning,* II, ii, 1, "Memorials are history unfinished, or the first or rough draughts of history"; and Dryden, *Aurungzebe*, v, i, 1195, "My Elder Brothers ...Rough draughts of Nature, ill design'd and lame."

19, 20. *For they as they have Life*, etc. This couplet is omitted in the *Parnassus Biceps.*

Page 46

LESBIA, ON HER SPARROW.

Cartwright is probably thinking of Skelton's *Phylyp Sparrow*; he was mildly interested in similar things, as we see, for example, from the language of Moth in *The Ordinary.* See also Gerber, *The Sources of Cartwright's Ordinary*, where the "Chaucerianisms" are traced home. The poem "is pretty and runs trippingly" according to the *Retrospective* reviewer who quotes it in full.

Page 47

THE GNAT.

7. *As warmer Jet doth ravish straws.* Sir Thos. Browne in his *Pseudodoxia Epidemica* (1646), Bk II, ch. lv, gives details. Fuller in his *Just Man's Funeral* (1649) speaks of "Jet memories only attracting straws and chaff unto them."

Page 48
A BILL OF FARE.

30. *Keckerman* (1573-1609) was a German scholar who systematized many branches of knowledge. He was evidently commonly regarded as a standard of intellectual subtlety. Overbury, in ridiculing the muddleheadedness of "A meer Scholar," says: "He will not sticke to averre that Systema's logicke doth excell Keckerman's." Keckerman's *Manuduction t Theology*, done into English by Thos. Vicars (1621?), contains a commendatory poem by Michael Drayton.

49. *For, if this Fasting hold*: cf. Introd. p. xii and footnote.

Page 50
THE CHAMBERMAID'S POSSET.

An inferior text may be found in *The Marrow of Compliments* (1653) in the Bodleian Library. The verses were possibly sung to the tune of *Cocklorrel*, a song very similar in both measure and substance to this.

3. *gravell'd*: nonplussed, as in the passage from *As You Like It*, IV, i, 74, "Nay, you were better speak first, and when you were gravelled for lack of matter you might take occasion to kiss." Again in Marlowe's *Faustus*, i, 114, "And I that have with concise syllogisms Gravell'd the pastors of the German church." The idea is obvious. A Frenchman, says Howell (*Instructions for Forraine Travell*, v), "is often gravelled upon the quicksands of his own braine."

9. *Sir John was resolved to suffer a Drench*. A drench (O.E. *drencan*, to make to drink) was usually a drink in the medicinal sense. But Ben Jonson speaks of another order of refreshment as "a drench of sack at a good tavern."

23. *Buchanan*, Geo.: the famous Scottish scholar (1506-82) and author of *Detectio Mariae Reginae*, 1571, an attack on Queen Mary, and of *De Jure Regni apud Scotos* (1579), directed against absolutism.

28. *Simpling*, i.e. concocting simples or herbal medicines. "The Brethren" and "The Sanctified Fraternity" were nicknames for the Puritan party. The doctrines of their numerous sects were indeed very variously "concocted."

30. *Histrio-mastix*, written in 1632 by William Prynne the Puritan pamphleteer, attacked stage plays. Cartwright detested all the Puritans; in *The Ordinary* (Act v, Sc. v) he identifies them with traitors and those agape for treason, and rejoices at their emigrations. Prynne was expelled from Oxford in 1634. An additional cause of irritation to Cartwright may have been Prynne's continual praise of that "other Mr Cartwright," referred to in this poem as T. C.

31. *T. C.* The usual signature of Thomas Cartwright (1538-

1603), one of the most intolerant of the Puritans. In 1572 appeared his *Admonitions to the Parliament* attacking the organisation of the English Church. He reinforced his thesis later in *A Second Admonition*. Whitgift published replies to both. Hooker's famous *Laws of Ecclesiastical Polity* (1592) comes at the conclusion of this controversy and aims to justify the English Church in its organised form.

In one of the introductory poems to the 1651 Edition of Cartwright, Monmouth contrasts Thomas the Puritan and William the Poet:

> Yet Cartwright makes amends by clear wit
> For all the Schisms the other Cartwright writ.

33. *Stript Whipt Abuses.* Geo. Wither (1588–1667), who in 1613 wrote the satire called *Abuses stript and whipt*, was a Puritan of a more than ordinary independence of mind. His egotistical satires went through many editions. Wither's *Motto* (1621) is prefixed by an "Embleme," with the superscription:

> Nec habeo, nec careo, nec curo.

The hero (himself?) is he who lacks worldly but not spiritual possessions, and fears no mere terrestrial assaults.

37. *Clever and Doddisme.* John Dod was Puritan rector of Fawsley, a notable "nonconformist" centre, from 1624. Richard Cleaver and he published several works together; among them the most remarkable was an exposition of the ten commandments, on account of which book Dod was popularly known as "Decalogue Dod."

39. *Discipline* and *Christian Liberty* (l. 48) were favourite Puritan expressions, useful in theological polemics. We hear of this "beauteous discipline" in *Bartholomew Fair*. Wither in his *Motto* (1621), referred to above, declares

> As much abhor I, brutish Vanities,
> As much allow I, Christian Liberties.

See also the poem *To Dr Duppa after the Publick Act*, l. 52, p. 20:

> This was their Christian Freedom here: nay we,
> Our selves too then, dur.t plead a Liberty.

49. There were many editions of *The Crums of Comfort*, a pious and non-partisan book of meditation and prayer. "A Prayer for God's protection of his Church in respect of the present Troubles in it" is an example of one of the prayers. The earliest edition in the British Museum (1628) is bound together with a volume of the *Psalms* of Sternhold and Hopkins.

53. *An Ell-London measure.* London merchants allowed something beyond the standard yard in their measurements.

59.   *The Glass was Compell'd still Rubbers to run,*
       And he counted the Fift Evangelist.

The modern technical sense of the word "Rubber" in connexion with card and other games is familiar enough; but its application is made more broadly here. It is the only example in this sense given by the *New English Dictionary*. The *Glass* is the pulpit timepiece.

61. *The Pig that for haste*, etc. The eyes of a pig roasted "to a turn" were supposed to drop out. There is a parallel passage in *To Dr Duppa after the Publick Act*, l. 61, p. 21.

67. *pouch'd*, i.e. pocketed. Hence it comes to mean "swallowed."

Page 53
ON A GENTLEWOMAN'S SILK HOOD.

There are texts of this poem preserved in MS. in the Bodleian (Malone MSS. 21) *an.* 1644, and in the Brit. Mus. (Addit. MSS. 1854-75, 22, 0061 ff, 16 *b*, 26 *b*). *The Marrow of Compliments* (1653), which is full of strange versions of Cartwright's poems, contains a strange distortion of some lines of this one, but in a different measure, as follows:

> *The presentation of a Sylke Hood.*
> So Love appear'd breaking his way
> When from the Chaos he brought day,
> Drawne from the tender bud, so showes
> The half seene glory of the Rose
> As you when veyl'd and I may sweare
> (Viewing your beauty) buddeth there.
> Such doubtful life had groves, where Rods
> And twigs at last did shoot up Gods,
> When shade then darkeneth the place.
> Accept this vaile then (sweet) for I
> Affect a clouded Deitee.

The poem has had to be changed to fit the "presentation"; the compiler of *The Marrow* seems to have recognized how Cartwright's verses outshone all others in the required spirit of exaggerated gallantry. Cf. the lines quoted above with:

> So Love appear'd when, breaking out his way
> From the dark Chaos, he first shed the day;
> Newly awak'd out of the Bud so shews
> The half seen, half-hid glory of the Rose.
> As you do through your Veyls.

The MS. versions read *So Jove appear'd*, but the above is the better reading. So in *Marriage of Lady Mary*, 1st stanza:

> Love from that Masse did leap;
> And what was but an Heap
> Rude and Ungatherd, swift as thought, was hurld
> Into the Beauty of an Ordred World.

The same ancient and popular philosophic notion is restated in Ben Jonson's *Masque of Beauty*:

> When Love at first did move
> From out of Chaos, brightned
> So was the world, and lightned
> As now...

Page 58

PARTHENIA FOR HER SLAIN ARGALUS.

Quarles's *Argalus and Parthenia*, a typical 17th century epyllion was published in 1629. It is interspersed with lyrics, one, e.g *Parthenia To Her Faithful Argalus*, in Book 1. "It was a siens taken out of the Orchard of Sir Philip Sidney," says Quarles. The incident in the *Arcadia* is related in a manner right romantic The "conjugall happiness" of Parthenia has been brought to an end by the combat between Amphialus and her husband, Argalus The latter is mortally wounded in the fight, when "the beautiful *Parthenia* (who had that night dreamed she sawe her husband in such estate, as she then founde him, which made her make such haste hither)...ran between them...*Parthenia*...bewrayled her self with so lamentable sweetnes, as was inough to have taught sorrow to the gladdest thoughts, and have engraved it in the mindes of hardest mettall. O *Parthenia*, no more *Parthenia* (said she) wha art thou?...O wandring life, to what wildernes wouldst thou lead me?....*Argalus*, *Argalus*, I wil folow thee[2]." Later, Amphialu is challenged by an unknown knight, whom he overthrows, and i about to kill, when "there fell about the shoulders of the overcome knight the treasure of faire golden haire, which with the face (soon known by the badge of excellencie) witnessed it was *Parthenia*, the unfortunatelie vertuous wife of Argalus." Amphialus offers her his aid. "But Parthenia (who had inward messengers of the desired deathes approch) looking upon him, and streight turning away her feeble sight, as from a delightlesse object, drawing out her wordes, which her breath (loath to part from so sweete a bodie did faintly deliver, Sir (saide she) I pray you (if prayers have place in enemies) to let my maides take my body untouched by you : the onely honour I now desire by your meanes, is, that I have no honour of you. *Argalus* made no such bargaine with you, that the hand which killed him, shoulde helpe me. I have of them (and I do not onely pardon you, but thank you for it) the service which I desired. There rests nothing now but that I go live with him since whose death I have done nothing but die[3]."

Page 59

ARIADNE DESERTED BY THESEUS, AS SHE SITS UPON A ROCK IN THE ISLAND NAXOS, THUS COMPLAINS.

This is the first song in Lawes' *Ayres and Dialogues* (1653) where a synopsis of the story, "as much as concerns the ensuing Relation," is given. This is probably the "story" referred to by Milton in his *Sonnet to Henry Lawes*:

Thou honour'st Verse, and Verse must lend her wing
To honour thee, the priest of Phoebus' quire
That tunest their happiest lines in hymn or story.

Some accounts tell us that Ariadne was killed in Naxos, some tha

---

[1] scion.   [2] *Arcadia*, III, 12.   [3] *Arcadia*, III, 16.

she committed suicide in despair. Others again, like the present poem, say that she was finally saved by Dionysus, who raised her among the gods. Cartwright's lines are also to be found in Nichol's *Collection of Poems*, I, 58.

31.
> *Till my Eyes drank up his,*
> *And his drank mine,*
> *I ne'r thought Souls might kiss,*
> *And Spirits joyn.*

Compare these lines with Cartwright's excellent poem *No Platonique Love* (p. 67):

> Tell me no more of minds embracing minds,
> And hearts exchang'd for hearts;
> That Spirits Spirits meet, as Winds do Winds,
> And mix their subt'lest parts;
> That two unbodi'd Essences may kiss,
> And then like Angels, twist and feel one Bliss.

In Castiglione (Hoby's translation of *The Book of the Courtier* appeared in 1561) one of the problems discussed is that of the true courtier in love. The solution, which is Platonic love, is enthusiastically praised. Elizabethan poetry is full of the idea. Says Bembo in *The Courtier*: "Sins the nature of man in youthful age is so much inclined to sense, it may be graunted the courtier, while he is young, to love sensuallye. But in case afterwarde also in hys riper years, he chaunse to be set on fire with this coveting of love, he ought to be good and circumspect...and first consider that the body, where that beautye shyneth, is not the fountaine from whens beauty springeth, but rather bicause beautie is bodilesse...she loseth much of her honoure whan she is coopled with that vile subject and full of corruption, bicause the lesse she is partner thereof the more perfect she is, and cleane sundred frome it, is most perfect." The Courtier by practising the love of ideal beauty can avoid the torment of the absence of the loved one. The mere sensual lover "loseth this treasure and happinesse, as soone as the woman beloved with her departure leaveth the eyes without their brightnes, and consequently the soule, as a widowe without her joye." References to the theme are found in nearly all the writers of this time. Thomas Stanley employs the motive freely in his poems, but, like Cartwright, has also the refusal:

> Forbear, Platonick fools, t'enquire
> What numbers do the soul compose.

Cartwright was thoroughly interested in the theme, which must have been a good deal discussed by the poets. Mr E. K. Chambers has a relevant note on Donne's (?) poem, "Soul's Joy, now I am gone."

He quotes a poem by Sir K. Digby, written after the death of Lady Digby in 1633.

> And I see those books are false which teach
> That absence works between two souls no breach
> When they with love to each other move,
> And that they (though distant) may meet, kiss and play.

Cartwright's *No Platonique Love* is a similar protest against the merely theoretic. Then there is Carew's (with which poet Cartwright has much in common) *To my Mistress in Absence*, e.g.:

> There, though our Bodies are Disjoin'd
> As things that are to place confin'd,
> Let our boundless spirits meet.

The discussion seems to have gained a new interest on account of some incident at Court. See the lines from the play by Sir Wm. Davenant, *The Platonic Lovers* (1636):

> Right Sir, the first are Lovers of a pure
> Celestiall kind, such as some stile Platonicall:
> (A new Court Epithet scarce understood)
> But all they wooe, Sir, is the Spirit, Face,
> And Heart, therefore their conversation is
> More safe to Fame, the others still affect
> For naturall ends.

See, also, Cowley's *The Mistress*. The exact date of the incident or revived interest at Court is best seen from one of the *Familiar Letters* of James Howell, viz. that to Mr Phillip Warwick at Paris (3rd June, 1634):

"The Court affords little news at present, but that there is a love called platonic love, which much sways there of late. It is a love abstracted from all corporal gross impressions and sensual appetite, but consists in contemplations and ideas of the mind, not in any carnal fruition. This love sets the wits of the town on fire, and they say there will be a mask shortly of it, whereof her Majesty and her maids of honour will be part."

Page 63

NO DRAWING OF VALENTINES.

1. 　　　　*Cast not in Chloe's Name among*
　　　　The common undistinguish'd Throng:

February 14th, St Valentine's Day. "It is a ceremony," says Bourne, "never omitted among the vulgar, to draw lots which they term Valentines, on the eve before Valentine Day. The names of a select number of one sex are by an equal number of the other put into some vessel, and after that everyone draws a name, which for the present is call'd their Valentine, and is looked upon as a good omen of their being man and wife afterward." V. also Brand's and Hazlitt's *Popular Antiquities*.

Page 67

NO PLATONIQUE LOVE.

V. Note *supra*. Cartwright's "*Tell* me no more" may have suggested Carew's "*Ask* me no more," which, however, is used to much fuller effect in Carew's famous song[1]. The relation between Carew

---

[1] See remarks in the Introduction (p. xxxi) with regard to the earliness in date of Cartwright's verses.

and Cartwright is interesting. They have many subjects in common:
perhaps they both worked at subjects given them by Ben Jonson.
The next poem *Absence*, for instance, has an opening similar to
Carew's

> Go, thou gentle whispering wind,
> Bear this sigh.

Cartwright's poem, *A Gnat mistaking her bright Eye*, corresponds to
Carew's *A fly that flew into my Mistress's Eye*. V. also note to
Ariadne, l. 31 *ante*.

17, 18. As Thomas Watson said: "Siquidem opinati sunt aliqui,
in osculo fieri animarum combinationem."

Page 68

CONSIDERATION.

1. *Fool that I was, that little of my Span*
    Which I have sinn'd untill it stil's me Man.

The poem touches a graver note, and acts as an introduction to the
more serious poems which follow. .

Page 69

UPON THE TRANSLATION OF CHAUCER'S TROILUS AND CRESEIDE BY SIR FRANCIS KYNASTON.

Sir Francis Kynaston (1587-1642) was the centre of a literary
coterie at the court of Charles I. In 1635 he founded an institution
of learning known as the Musaeum Minervae. His *Amores Troili
et Cresseidae* appeared in 1635 and was prefaced by fifteen poems by
Oxford writers. The best text of this poem is to be found there.

Page 70

GROTIUS' ELEGY ON ARMINIUS.

Cartwright probably took his Latin text from *Hugonis Grotii
Poemata* published in London 1639. The poem occurs in Book III
(No. 6).

Page 74

MARTIAL Lib. I. Epig. 66.

1. *Th'art out, vile Plagiary*, the last couplet of which:
    > He that repeats stoln Verse, and for Fame looks,
    > Must purchase Silence too as well as Books,

is quoted by the writer of the preface to the 1651 edition. This
epigram is numbered 67 in the 1651 edition. Thomas May
"Englished" selected epigrams from Martial in 1629, and epigrams
of the sort became extremely common. Martial was a favourite
with Ben Jonson who recommended him to Drummond of Haw-
thornden.

8. *Not slubber'd yet by any ruffer Chin*: i.e. sullied or smeared.

Page 76

MARTIAL. Lib. ii, Epig. 18 (*not* 19).

9. *Cosmus Leaf*: "cosmi folium." Some editors read "costi folium," "Leaf of spikenard," but "spikenard," says Bohn, "does not grow in Italy."

20. *for when thou didst bestow*
This Mead confirm'd unto me by thy Seal
I'd rather far th'hadst given me a Meal.

Mead....Meal, in the Latin: *praedium...prandium.*

Page 77

HORAT. CARM. Lib. iv. Ode 13.

The Quarterly Review, clxxx, 121, quotes "one stanza (and that not the best)" from Cartwright's "admirable version" of *Audivere Lyre.* The stanza quoted is the one beginning:

Thou wert a while the cry'd-up Face.

4. *Putt'st in for handsome still*, i.e. "claimest to be"; so in modern colloquial speech.

19. *Neither thy Coan Purples lay*: in the Latin, "nec Coae... purpurae."

Page 78

ON THE BIRTH OF THE KING'S FOURTH CHILD.

The Princess Elizabeth, born December 28th, 1635. The text of these verses is taken from the University address *Coronae Carolinae quadratura* of which there is no copy in the British Museum. In this book there are three distinct poems not quite patently by the same author. The third, which comes at the end of the *Coronae*, is unsigned. However, they are all published together in the 1651 edition.

Page 79

THE SAME.

27. *Some, their owne Plagiaries, will be read*
In the Elder statue with a younger Head.

"Marcellus was accused for taking off Augustus his head, and putting the head of Tiberius upon the same statue."—A note by Cartwright in the 1651 edition.

30. *Chronogramme.* The phrase "LorD haVe MerCIe Vpon Vs" is a chronogram for the year 1666. The example is from *The Athenaeum*, No. 28.

Page 81

TO MRS DUPPA.

Duppa became Bishop of Chichester in 1638. In 1660 (nine years after the publication of the collected poems of Cartwright) he became Bishop of Winchester. Cartwright's devotion to his patron is apparent from these verses. He sees the signs of coming unrest (cf. Stanza 4) but trusts in the foresight of his leader.

2. *in half a quarrell*: i.e. "the small peece of Glass." So in Puttenham's *English Poesie*: "The Lozenge is...a quadrangle reverst with his point upward like to a quarrell of glasse." Spenser uses the word for the bolt of the cross-bow (*Faerie Queen*, II, xi, 24).

71. *your Church*, i.e. Christ Church, Oxford, to which Duppa made many munificent bequests.

Page 84
TO THE KING, ETC.

The 1651 edition has a wrong title for this poem, viz. "To the king, on the birth of the Princess Elizabeth." The poems of the *Flos Britannicus...Filiola* series, from which this is taken, celebrate the birth of Princess Anne, who was born March 17th, 1636-7. The little princess died in 1640.

Cartwright also contributed a Latin poem to the series.

22. *Five glasses*. The children of Henrietta were, in order: Charles II, born 29th May, 1630; Mary, Princess of Orange, 4th Nov. 1631; James II, 14th October, 1633; Elizabeth, 28th Jan. 1635-6; Anne, 17th March, 1636-7.

30. *the Golden Chain's let downe again*. The well-known allusion in Homer (*Iliad*, VIII, 19) to the rope of gold which bound Heaven and Zeus with all on earth has been interpreted in many different allegorical ways. Chaucer refers to "that faire cheyne of love" in *The Knight's Tale* (2183) and elsewhere. The references might be multiplied. Ben Jonson, speaking of the binding rites of marriage, makes "Reason" declare

> Such was the golden chain let down from heaven,
> And not those links more even
> Than these: so sweetly tempered, so combined
> By union and refined.

Other well-known references are in Bacon (*Advancement of Learning*, I, § 2, and elsewhere) and Spenser (*Faerie Queene*, I, V, 25).

Page 86
TO THE QUEEN.

3. *For wee, who have not wit propitious, doe*
Travell with verse, and feele our Braine-pangs too.

Similarly, in the verses *On the Birth of the King's Fourth Child*, l. 5, "We aemulous too Bring forth, and with more pangs perhaps than You."

Page 87
MR JOHN FLETCHER.

These two commendatory poems by Cartwright appeared amongst others in the 1647 collection of the *Comedies and Tragedies, written by Francis Beaumont and John Fletcher, Gentlemen*. His first poem is there entitled *Upon the Report of the Printing of the Dramaticall Poems of Master John Fletcher*.

5.   *Who therefore wisely did submit each birth*
    To knowing Beaumont e're it did come forth.

Aubrey states that Beaumont's "main business was to correct the over-flowings of Mr Fletcher's witte." "Beaumont's judgment checked what Fletcher writ" (Pope). See the Essay by G. C. Macaulay, 1883, on this topic.

15. *his Shepheardess*: *The Faithful Shepherdess*, most famous of English pastoral plays, was the unaided work of Fletcher.

21.   *A piece, which Johnson in a rapture bid*
    Come up a glorifi'd work and so it did.

Jonson said his poem would "rise"

      A glorified work to time, when fire
Or moths shall eat what all these fools admire.

(Ben Jonson: *To Mr John Fletcher, upon his "Faithful Shepherdess."*)

Page 89

ANOTHER ON THE SAME.

33. *Where we see 'twas not chance that made them hit*: i.e. hit the mark, succeed. So in Dryden's *Essay upon Satire*:

    Sometimes he has some humour, never wit,
    And if it rarely, very rarely, hit,
    'Tis under so much nasty rubbish hid,
    To find it out's the cinderwoman's trade.

35. *Dürer* (1471–1528), the great German painter and engraver of Nuremberg, paid a good deal of attention to the study of perspective. His *Elementa Geometrica* was first published in 1532 and went through many editions. It was found suitable as a text-book of perspective, and his seventeenth century fame in this respect is proved from the *Albert Dürer Revived* (1660), a practical treatise for students of drawing, and giving a "portraiture" of Dürer, the "verie prime painter and graver of Germany."

44. *That they (their own Black Friers) unacted breath*: referring to the playhouse of that name that stood between Ludgate Hill and the Thames, pulled down in 1655.

69. *Shakespeare to thee was dull, whose best jest lyes*
    I'th' Ladies questions, and the Fooles replyes.
    Old fashion'd wit, etc.

These famous lines and the preceding judgment on Ben Jonson are valuable for the history of criticism, valuable because they are discerning and reasonable, because, too, of the fame of the critic. We see from the lines quoted how the Elizabethan imagination was out of date for "correct" poets: though Cartwright will yet concede that Shakespeare was certainly capable of good clownish repartee, simple natural human stuff. It is a point of view; and I am reminded of an Indian student who recorded similar and somewhat refreshing "first impressions of Shakespeare." "Shakespeare's humorous characters," he wrote, "reveal great truths in the form of witty and amusing remarks. These amusing remarks and repartees are full of interest."

(V. Courthope, *Hist. of Eng. Poetry*, Vol. IV, Ch. 2, and *Caml*. *Hist. of Eng. Lit.*, Vol. VII, Ch. 3, where these lines are quoted.)

Page 92

TO THE RIGHT REVEREND ... BRIAN, LORD BISHOP OF CHICHESTER.

Probably written in 1638 on Duppa's appointment to the see of Chichester. Cartwright's signature to the poem was as follows: "The most faithful Honourer of Your Lordships vertues W. C."

57. *And for his Charg's Birth-sake, May*
     Shall be to me one Holy Day.

Charles was born on the 29th of May, 1630.

114. *Thistles*, i.e. Scotland. There is a note to this effect in the margin of the 1651 edition.

137. *As that learn'd Man, who Hazell pill'd,*
     And so by Art his own Flock fill'd.

Pilled is cognate with *peeled*. "And Jacob took him rods of...hazel... and pilled white strakes in them...And the flocks conceived before the rods, and brought forth cattle ringstraked, speckled, and spotted (*Genesis* xxx. 37, 39).

Page 100

A NEW-YEAR'S GIFT TO DUPPA.

There is a notable change of kind in these and the verses which follow. The account in the Preface to the 1651 edition may be exaggerated ("here is nothing his Function need blush at...but one sheet written after he entered Holy Orders"), but there was evidently a true and thorough change in his manner of life.

Duppa is here addressed as the Bishop of Sarum, although the poem is dated 1638. He was promoted from Chichester to Salisbury in 1641 (see p. 179).

Page 102

TO THE QUEEN, AFTER HER DANGEROUS DELIVERY, 1638.

"The infant princess Catherine (born and died Jan. 29th, 1638-9), who is commemorated in these verses, seems to have lived a few hours only, and to be unnoticed in ordinary pedigrees and histories" (Madan). The verses were entitled *Musarum Oxoniensium... Charisteria fro...Maria*, Ox. 1638. Cartwright has a Latin poem also among the contributions.

29. *Thus stood Horatius*: Note in the *Charisteria*, but omitted in 1651 edition: "*Liv. Decad.* 1. lib. 2."

Page 104

ON THE DEATH OF ... VISCOUNT BAYNING.

Paul Bayning became heir to the Viscounty of Sudbury in 1629.
He died July 11th, 1638, without heirs, the title becoming extinct.

*Death repeat'd by a thankful Memorial sent from Christ Church
in Oxon* (Lord Bayning's college), was published soon afterwards
(Ox. 1638). All the contributors were Oxford men and included
Will Strode, orator of the University, Will Burton and Cartwright
Fasti, I, 468).

20. *Loose Italian Vices,* the Italian styles of dressing and living
standing for all that was evil to the 17th century. There are many
English translations, for example, of the Italian proverb "Inglese
Italianato è un diavolo incarnato."

43. *Who could e're say my Lord, and the next Marsh
Made frequent Herriots?*

The heriot (O.E. *here-geatve*) is the present or feudal service due
to the overlord on the removal or death of a tenant. As a good
landlord, his tenants were likely to remain with him and prosper.
The O.E. word occurs in the *Battle of Maldon,* l. 48:

þā heregeatu þe ēow æt hilde ne ðeah.

Page 106

TO BEN JONSON.

This was Cartwright's contribution to the collection of verses
—*Jonsonus Virbius,* Lond. 1638—collected by friends of Ben Jonson
after his death. Hence is taken the text of the poem as here
printed. The latter half (from "No rotten talke") is quoted in *The
Retrospective Review.* The whole poem is given by Nichol (*Collection
of Poems,* p. 63) together with an outline-sketch of Cartwright's
life.

83. *brokes:* i.e. bargains for. Cf. l. 85, "No bargaining line
there."

122. *Low without creeping.* "Denham undoubtedly had these
lines in his mind in the famous passage from *Cooper's Hill.* Cartwright died in 1643, the same year in which Denham's poem was
printed; but that the latter was the copy, had there been room
for doubt of date, is proved by their superior elegance of expression"
(*Notes and Queries,* IV, 4, 511, by "J. A. G."). Denham entered
Trinity College, Oxford, in 1631. The first edition of *Cooper's Hill*
was published in 1642, but does not contain the lines in question.
These are:

> O could I flow like thee, and make thy stream
> My great example as it is my theme!
> Though deep, yet clear; though gentle, yet not dull;
> Strong without rage; without o'er flowing, full.

The lines appeared in the second edition (1654), soon after the
publication of Cartwright's collected poems. They are the best

remembered of all Denham's verses; it is therefore important to know that Cartwright was not the plagiarist.

150. *Fit*: cf. *supra*, note to l. 33, *Another on the same*, p. 195, *supra*.

171. *Porcelaine-wit.* Cartwright thinks that the wit of Jonson is careful, delicate and finished like porcelaine. Mr Birrell (*Obiter Dicta*) speaks of "delicate porcelain opinions." Sir Thomas Browne (*Pseudodoxia Epidemica*, II, v) refers to the common belief "that porcelain or china dishes...are made of earth, which lieth in preparation about an hundred years under ground." So Donne, in his *Elegie on the Lady Marckham*:

> As men of China, after an ages stay,
> Do take up Porcelane, where they buried Clay...

Page 115

UPON THE BIRTH OF THE KING'S SIXTH CHILD.

I.e. Prince Henry, born July 8th, 1640. The full title of the series to which this belongs, together with another Latin poem by Cartwright, was *Horti Carolini Rosa Altera*.

63. *This Floating Island.* The other "floating island" was Delos, which became "setled," i.e. made suddenly visible, according to the old legend. Cf. Spenser, *Faerie Queene*, II, xii, 13.

Page 117

ON THE DEATH OF LORD STAFFORD.

Printed in *Honour and Virtue, Triumphing over, the Grave...Life and Death of 'Henry' Lord Stafford*, by Anthony Stafford (London, 1640). The book was "much embelish'd by the addition of many most elegant elegies penned by the most acute wits of these times." Cartwright's poem comes second, following that of John Beaumont. There is another version of the poem in the *Parva sus Biceps* (1656).

Anthony Stafford (b. 1587), the author of *The Female Glory*, died, according to Wood, during the Civil wars. He was himself an Oxford man, and a relative of the Lord Henry. The latter succeeded his grandfather and to the title in 1602, but "died unmarried in October, 1637...The barony devolved upon his brother Roger, who, on account of his poverty, illegally resigned the dignity to Charles I for £800. Roger died without issue in 1640, but some male descendants of the family are said still to survive in humble circumstances." See accounts under *Anthony Stafford* and *Henry Stafford, first Baron Stafford*, in the *Dict. of Nat. Biography*.

27. *Had he then liv'd.* This passage (up to l. 44, "*Instruments and Men*") is omitted in *Honour and Virtue*, though the poem appears in full in the 1651 edition, followed by Chalmers.

Page 121

TO MR THOMAS KILLIGREW ON HIS TWO PLAYES, *THE PRISONERS AND CLARACILLA.*

The Prisoners and *Claracilla* by Tho. Killigrew Gent. were published in 1641; the text is taken from that book. Thos. Killigrew was born in 1612 and died in 1683. In 1633 he was page to Charles I. Both these plays were performed before 1636.

35. *No Thrifty Spare, or Manage of dispence.* The term "manage" was commonly used in connexion with the training of a horse, as in Spenser (*Faerie Queene*, II, iv, 1) and in Shakespeare (1 *Henry IV*, II, iii, 52). But Cartwright gives the word a wider application—it occurs again in *An Epitaph on Mr Poultney*, l. 8—and r ther in the French sense of government and economy in affairs.

49. *Or as the Elephant breeds*, etc. "The vulgar notion is that the elephant goes with young ten years" (Pliny).

Page 123

ON THE MARRIAGE OF LADY MARY TO THE PRINCE OF ORANGE HIS SON, MAY 2, 1641.

The Princess Mary, eldest daughter of Charles I, was then not yet ten years old.

The best text is from the academic collection known as the *Proteleia Anglo-Batava*.

57. *zone.* Corrected in Errata (1651 edition) from *tone.*

Page 126

TO THE EARL OF PEMBROKE.

Elected Chancellor July 1st, 1641. This poem, published as a broadside, is in the Luttrell Collection (Brit. Mus. No. 120).

The following is listed in the *Catalogue of the Valuable Library of B. H. Bright.* No. 1042. "Cartwright (Will.). *Secunda Vox Populi*, or, the Commons gratitude to Philip Earl of Pembroke, for the great affection which he alwaies bore them, a Poem. Woodcut portrait 4to. 1641." Hazlitt distinguishes two books, as follows:

Vox Secunda Populi, or, the Commons gratitude (as above), by Thomas Herbert, and

Secunda Vox Populi, etc. With some verses upon his Lordship's Election of Chancellor of the University of Oxford, by William Cartwright.

Thomas Herbert (1597–1642?) was the youngest brother of Lord Herbert of Cherbury and of George the poet. J. M. Rigg (Article, "Thomas Herbert," *D.N.B.*) gives among the list of his poems: "*Vox Secunda Populi*…with verses by *Thomas* Cartwright appended to some copies." In the British Museum copy, following the address to the Earl, comes a verse-dedication of eighteen lines, signed by Thomas Herbert. The poem itself is unsigned. The writer seems to be Herbert, however, a "vassall" of the Earl, and he refers to his own words more than once as standing for the "Vox Populi."

The only verses to Pembroke by Cartwright that are in the British Museum are those in the broadside above referred to. The lines are headed by a woodcut trll-length portrait of the Earl, similar to that in the *Vox Secunda.*

The question is a difficult one. *Thomas* Cartwright in the *D.N.B.* must be a misprint. Perhaps Cartwright's effusion on the election may have become known as the "*Secunda" Vox Populi,* and, in some unknown edition, the two panegyrics were printed together.

Page 129

EPITAPH ON MR POULTNEY.

This is quoted by *The Retrospective Review* which describes the poem as "sensible, feeling and concise."

Page 135

TO THE MEMORY OF SIR HENRY SPELMAN

(1564–1641).

The well-known historian and antiquary. His *History of Sacrilege* was not published until 1698. He compiled, too, a glossary of Latin and Anglo-Saxon Law Terms. In 1635 he wrote a letter to a friend at Cambridge about founding an Anglo-Saxon lectureship there. He was buried in Westminster Abbey, 1641 Cartwright himself was interested in the study of the English language. Gerber has shown this in his thesis, *The Sources of Cartwright's Ordinary.*

3. *Exprobration,* i.e. holding up to rebuke. So in Cartwright's play *The Siedge,* II, vi, "He shall...avoi! thy sight...as something that doth exprobate His sins unto him."

20. *Ahaz Diall:* 2 Kings xx. 11.

46. *Witness that Chantorie Piece that lights Our Corps to a bought Graces,*

that is, his *De Sepulture,* treating of the custom of paying for burial ground. The money, according to Spelman, "was first given for praying for Souls and such like, but that being abolished and given to the king, the Parsons, it seemeth, take it for the Grave.'

Page 140

THE QUEEN'S RETURN.

This poem was first published in the *Musarum Oxoniensium... Epibateria...Mariae ex Batavia Feliciter Reduci,* Ox. 1643[1]. Cartwright signs this poem as junior proctor; he only became proctor

<hr>

[1] This series is not mentioned in Madan's *Catalogue of Oxford Books.*

in April, and the Queen landed in February. The second and fifth stanzas are deleted in most of the 1651 editions, censured as too royalist. The Grenville copy contains the missing parts, and the phrase "for the King's own good" is italicized. The reference was to the cannonade fired on the Queen at her landing in Burlington. One of the Parliamentary captains responsible for this was seized and condemned, but graciously pardoned by the Queen. He was so touched by this kindness that he and several comrades came over to the King's side. Hence the episode was "for the King's own good" (v. Strickland, *Lives of the Queens of England*, Vol. v).

13. *Courage was cast.* The succeeding four "beautiful lines of Cartwright" are quoted in *The Quarterly Review* (xiii, 488) from a life of Wellington, and there applied to the behaviour of the Duchess of Angoulême at Waterloo, "who, on that frightful occasion, displayed so royal, so heroic a spirit."

25. *Look on Her Enemies*, etc. There has been some question as to what these lines refer. It is definitely stated by one writer (in *Notes and Queries*, First Series, i, 108, 151) that the authorship of the whole of this poem is doubtful owing to the date of Cartwright's death. He proceeds to argue that, at any rate, this fifth stanza was the work of another hand, as referring to events that did not occur till years later. But the "Crown-Martyr" was, of course, not the King, but the Earl of Strafford, executed on May 12th, 1641.

Page 142
UPON THE DEATH OF THE RIGHT VALIANT
SIR BEVILL GRENVILL, KNIGHT.

Sir Bevill Grenville, who was a grandson of the Commander of the *Revenge*, was born in Cornwall in 1596. He went to Exeter College, Oxford, became a close friend of Sir John Eliot, and assisted at the latter's popular re-election to Parliament. He himself was a member of both the Short and Long Parliaments. He accompanied Charles against the Scots in 1639 and so obtained his knighthood. He opposed the death of Strafford and did not sign the Protestation. In February, 1643, at the outbreak of the war, he wrote to his wife: "God's will be done. I am satisfied I cannot expire in a better cause." He was at the Royalist victory at Stratton, May, 1643, but was killed at Lansdown on July 5th. "The bloody and tedious battle lasted from break of day until very late at night, when Sir Beville Grenville, bravely behaving himself, was killed at the head of his stand of pikes."

In 1643 *Verses on the death of the right valiant Sir Beville Grenville* were published by the University of Oxford. Grenville was called "the Bayard of the West."

81. The lines from *You now that boast the Spirit and its sway* to *Cause* (l. 92) are omitted in the majority of the 1651 editions as being too anti-Puritan to be made public. They are present, however, in the Grenville copy in the British Museum (v. Bliss, *Ath. Ox.* Vol. iii, 72). The University verses were published in 1643 and

reprinted at London in 1684. Both original and reprint are in the British Museum.

90. *Traytor.* This was supposed (by a writer in *Notes and Queries*) to be Cromwell, but, as was pointed out, it was more probably either Waller or Essex. *Traytor* in the 1684 reprint fills the blank of the earlier editions.

Page 146
ON THE DEATH OF MRS ASHFORD.

1. *So when the great Elixar...th' Alembicks were...... biles h n i e do Lose not the Stone, but the Alembick too.* Cartwright never feels the dullness of continued repetition, even of so artificial and conventional a metaphor.

6. *Not known by it's Virtue so much as his Loss.* A second "by" before "Loss" would destroy the metre, but the line, as it stands falls away badly after the first half.

78. *Passions like Wilder Beasts thus tamed be.* Lloyd may have had these lines in his mind when writing his encomium on Cartwright's powers of oratory (v. Intro. p. xvii).

Page 149
NOVEMBER.

This may be the poem referred to in the preface to the 1651 edition: "And ... there's nothing kept from you but only one short paper of verses; what that is, and why it is not here, we need not tell you, for it hath been twice already Printed, though above our Power to bring it with its fellows." *November* was printed as a broadside in 1643, and was rather too Royalist in sympathy to bear reprinting in 1651. The poem was reprinted in 1671 at Oxford. The broadside is not mentioned by Madan in his lists of early Oxford printed books; neither is the poem to Sir B. Grenvill, likewise reprinted later. Both versions of the broadside are in the Bodleian, and have marginal commentaries. *November* is not given under "Cartwright" in the British Museum catalogue, but is among the Thomason Tracts. The 1643 commentaries are:

Stanza i. 3. *Departed Saints and Souls.* "First Day: All Saints; Second Day: All Souls."

Stanza ii. "Third Day: The Assembling of the Unhappy Parliament."

Stanza iii. "Fourth Day: The Birth of the Princess Mary."

Stanza iv. "Fifth Day: Our Delivery from the Papists' Conspiracy."

Stanza v. "Twelfth Day: The King's Victory at Brainford."

Stanza vi. "Sixteenth Day: The Birth of our gracious Queen Mary."

Stanza vii. "Seventeenth Day: The Beginning of Queen Elizabeth's Raigne."

Stanza viii. "Nineteenth Day: The Birth of our Gracious Prince Charles."

NOTES ON SONGS FROM THE PLAYS

Page 154

THE LADY ERRANT.

"The plot of *The Lady Errant* is even more fanciful [than that of *The Royal Slave*]; it is in part a reproduction of the fancy of a woman's commonwealth already made familiar to the stage by Fletcher's *The Sea Voyage*; but the character of the Lady Errant herself is not very intelligible, and the conduct of the whole action by no means dramatically effective" (Ward).

Page 155

VENUS AND ADONIS.

1. *Wake, my Adonis* (Act III, Sc. iv). This song, set to music by Dr Colman is found in the 1669 book of *Ayres and Dialogues*. Another version—*Venus lachrimans*—is to be found in *Parnassus Biceps* (1656).

2. *for thee and I* requires somewhat ample poetic license. This confusion between the nominative and objective cases of the personal pronoun is frequently found even in the politest of 16th and 17th century literature. Milton, for example, uses "Ye" in this way quite indiscriminately throughout *Areopagitica*. Compare

> To part with thee I needs must die,
> Could parting sep'rate thee and I,

from the poem *To Mrs A. at parting* by Katherine Philips, where indeed there is an antithetic effect that goes to justify her grammar. Cartwright was a Gloucestershire man, and there are country people there to-day who would find the grammar unexceptionable.

Page 157

THE EPILOGUE.

15. The *Kingdoms* are those of Cyprus and Crete.

28. *Cyprus*, where the scene is laid.

Page 158

THE ROYAL SLAVE

"Tells the adventures of an Ephesian, who, when a prisoner at the Persian Court, is 'adorned with all the Robes of Majesty' and invested with 'all Privileges for three full days, that he may do what he will, and then certainly be led to death.' Within these three days his heroic courage and magnanimity converts King Arsamnes into an admiring friend and ally" (Ward). Two editions of the play (1638 and 1640) are preserved both in the British Museum and the Bodleian Libraries. The better text, and that used in the 1651 edition, is from the second edition.

Page 160

PROLOGUE TO THE KING AND QUEEN.

"The first Appearance a Temple of the Sun. One of the Persian Magi discover'd in a Temple worshipping the Sun, at the sight of a new Majesty leaves the Altar, and addresseth himself to the Throne."

Page 161

THE PRIEST'S SONG.

This song is set to music in *Ayres and Dialogues*, 1669.

Page 162

LOVE AND MUSIC.

The music and the words of this song were published by Lawes in his *Ayres and Dialogues*, Book I, 1653. The title *Love and Music* is taken from Lawes. The first verse is also given in the 1669 volume of *Ayres* and reprinted in Beloe's *Anecdotes*, as is the first verse also of the foregoing *Come from the Dungeon*. All these songs were evidently very popular. *Come, my sweet* and *Now, now, the Sun is fled* also appear in inferior versions in *A Marrow of Compliments*.

Page 163

SONG

Now, now the Sun: quoted by Beloe.

Page 167

THE ORDINARY.

Here Cartwright "undertook to essay a picture of real life in Jonson's manner; but he confesses in the Prologue that he has only obtained his materials at second hand. A flimsy plot serves as the opportunity for revealing the ways of life of a gang of rascals, ruffians and tricksters, the scum of London society, who use a the centre of their operations a dining club at a tavern—the 'Ordinary' which gives its name to the play. Jonson was the model whom Cartwright followed in passages [as in the dinner scene *Ord.* II, i, cf. Jonson's *Alchemist,* I, i] as well as in the general conception of the Comedy....The play abounds in satire against the Puritans" (Ward).

28. *That is hight good fellow Robin.* In Jonson's masque of *Love Restored* he makes Robin Goodfellow say: "Would I had kept me to my gambols o' the country still, selling of fish, short service, shoeing the wild mare, or roasting of robin redbreast. I have recovered myself now for you, I am the honest plain country spirit, and harmless; Robin Goodfellow, he that sweeps the hearth and the house clean, riddles for the country maids, and does all their other drudgery..."

Page 168

LOVE ADMITS NO DELAY.

This song, set to music by Henry Lawes, was reprinted in the 1669 *Ayres and Dialogues.* There is a MS. version of the poem (MS. Rawl. D. 1092) in the Bodleian. The song is sung in the play by Priscilla, the lady's maid; hence *he* in line two is correct.

Page 169

THE SONG OF THE ORDINARY CLUBBERS.

Viz. "Vicar Catchmey, A Cathedral Singing Man; Bagshot, A Decay'd Clerk; Rimewell, A Poet; Sir Christopher, A Curate." Each takes a verse in turn.

7. *Mooting*: from the Old English *motung,* a term used at the Inns of Court for a legal discussion. "John of the Oak" and "John of the Stile" are the opposing parties in the mock case. *French* refers to the cockney cant language.

20. *Bellarmine.* Robert Bellarmine (1542–1621), Cardinal, Jesuit, and a theological writer of a remarkably tolerant and learned kind, was the author of many famous tracts in religious polemics. A *Bellarmine* was apparently a cant term for a large drinking-vessel. So in the *Ordinary:*

> Thou'rt like the larger jug, that some men call
> A Bellarmine, but we a Conscience;
> Whereon the lewder hand of pagan workman,
> Over the proud ambitious head, hath carved
> An idol huge, with beard episcopal,
> Making the vessel look like tyrant Eglon.

22. *Sutcliff*: Doctor Matthew Sutcliff, Dean of Exeter (1550?–1629), founded and endowed at Chelsea a college for the study and propagation of theological doctrines.

Page 171

SONG (Act IV. Sc. VI.)

Quoted in *A Marrow of Compliments* (1658), as "A Blessing Bestowed upon the Bantling of a Brownist."

3. *Dod's*: John Dod the Puritan; v. note above.

Page 172

THE EPILOGUE

is spoken by Shape, a "Cheater." The emigration of the Puritans became so general that in 1635 it was forbidden by proclamation.

THE SIEDGE, OR LOVE'S CONVERT.

"Borrows part of its plot from a not very impressive anecdote related of Pausanias by Plutarch in his *Life of Cimon*." Cartwright quotes Amyot's French as introduction to his play.] "According to the adaptation of the story given in the play, Leucasia, a virgin of Byzantium, is sent as a sacrifice to the tyrant Misander, whom her father has persuaded her to kill in his slumbers, but on suddenly awaking he stabs her while she is withdrawing irresolute.... The remainder of the play is occupied in the conversion of the tyrant into a virtuous lover by means of Leucasia's eloquence" (Ward).

Page xxxiii, Footnote 2.

It undeniably was a "new" fashion in poetry, and differed in many ways, if not radically, from the conceited mannerisms of Lyly or of Browne; and again from earlier and later fashions of affected writing on the continent.

Printed in the United States
137332LV00005B/12/P

9 781443 707671